BODY
AND
SOUL

BODY AND SOUL

gestalt therapy
and religious experience

JAMES LYNWOOD WALKER

Nashville • ABINGDON 𝄞 PRESS • New York

BODY AND SOUL

Copyright © 1971 by Abingdon Press

ISBN 0-687-03634-8

Library of Congress Catalog Card Number: 74-148077

Scripture quotations unless otherwise noted are from the Revised
Standard Version of the Bible, copyrighted 1946 and 1952 by
the Division of Christian Education, National Council of
Churches, and are used by permission.

Excerpts from *Suicide and the Soul* by James Hillman are copyright © 1964 by James Hillman. Reprinted by permission of
Harper & Row, Publishers, Inc.

Lines from *Inscape*, by Ross Snyder, are copyright © 1968 by
Abingdon Press. Used by permission of the publisher.

Appendixes E and G are excerpts from *Gestalt Therapy* by Frederick Perls, Ralph F. Hefferline, and Paul Goodman, The Julian
Press, Inc., 1951. Paperback edition, Delta, 1965.

Excerpts from *Religions, Values, and Peak Experiences* by Abraham Maslow, Ohio State University Press, 1964, are used by permission of the copyright owner, Kappa Delta Pi, an Honor Society
in Education.

Excerpts are reprinted by permission of the publisher from an
essay by John Enright in *Gestalt Therapy Now*, edited by Joen
Fagan and Irma Shepherd. Science and Behavior Books, Palo Alto,
Calif., 1970.

SET UP, PRINTED, AND BOUND BY THE
PARTHENON PRESS, AT NASHVILLE,
TENNESSEE, UNITED STATES OF AMERICA

To my wife, Harmon
significant partner in an
ever-changing gestalt

FOREWORD —————————————————

Roy W. Fairchild, Ph.D.,
Professor of Education
and Social Psychology,
San Francisco Theological
Seminary, and the Grad-
uate Theological Union

The late Alexander Miller of Stanford used to tell his students that the Old Testament had a "lip-smacking appreciation
of creation." So too this book. Its author, Lyn Walker, a
teacher at the Graduate Theological Union in Berkeley, has
spoken to the schizoid world of our day; a world which is out
of touch with vitality, aliveness, and meaning; a world which
has betrayed the body. Clergymen, pastoral counselors, psy-
chotherapists, and reflective laymen who want a sense of
wholeness in their lives and in their work will find it to be a
powerful tool for integrating their religious and psychological
understandings of life. The death-in-life existence of our time
cries out for new understandings of redemption. Through

7

the insights of Gestalt therapy, developed by the late Fritz
Perls (the book contains an excerpt from an unpublished interview with him), we are led into a new appreciation of
Judaic affirmation of the bodily life and the intimate bond
between man and earth. As one ponders these insights, he is
reminded of the title of a book written by the Quaker Rufus
Jones. *The Church's Debt to Heretics.* It is a debt that the
author cheerfully acknowledges.

As a pastoral counselor and teacher of psychology and education, I have profited from this book in many ways. I would
like to mention a few of its values by asking some of the
questions to which it speaks so cogently:

Why do we see the striking contrast between the promise
of aliveness in religious experience and the deadness of
people in the churches, including clergymen?

How do we protect ourselves from being deeply moved by
anything?

What is the result of the Protestant-inspired, "no-touch"
culture in which many of us have grown up?

Is there a way of fully experiencing anger, grief, sexuality,
and joy without losing control of ourselves?

Does a return to a Hebraic view of the body give us a new
way of understanding and facilitating religious experience?

Can counseling and psychotherapy be reconceived as a
way of exorcising the demonic in our lives?

Does one feel alive and real to the extent that he feels his
body to be alive and real?

This is a sample of the kind of questions explored in this
book. Anyone who wrestles with its conceptions will suffer a
blow to many of his familiar ideas of the religious life, but
he will grow in the process. I did. As expressed in the well-
known metaphor, many people live in only one room of their

house, while the house might actually be a palace with towers, banquet halls, sitting rooms, and gardens. They lock themselves in the kitchen or the cellar, believing this room to be the whole house. For them, this book may well be a key to an expanded life-space.

FOREWORD

JOHN B. ENRIGHT, PH.D.,
GESTALT THERAPIST,
CORTE MADERA, CALIFORNIA

Many of us who worked closely with Frederick S. Perls
(Fritz), the primary developer of Gestalt therapy, have re-
gretted his use of the word "therapy." I prefer such names as
the Gestalt *point of view*, the Gestalt *way of interacting*, the
Gestalt *style* or *approach*. All of life, not just the narrow and
grim domain of problems and symptoms, is the field of application of the Gestalt way. The early Gestalt psychologists saw
and explored the idea that the world, the "object" of perception, was best considered as a whole (gestalt), rather than a
collection of piecemeal parts. Fritz took the next step: I, the
perceiver, should also be whole and deal with all of the world
with all of me. If I am to be fully alive in the world, instead
of being static (dead) and detached from it, I must touch,
taste, smell, and push against the "object," rather than just
look from a distance. I must identify with it, be moved by

11

it, love it, or hate it, rather than just register or understand it; and I must paint, dance, sing, and act it to others, rather than merely talk about it. Thus, in my own life, I have greatly deepened my appreciation of painting, poetry, and nature through the Gestalt approach, and clarified some philosophical and epistemological problems. Each new possibility for living and using the Gestalt way excites me.

This is what Lyn Walker has done for me in this book; he has laid out a new field in which to experience the Gestalt way in action. Not a totally new field, of course; the relation of man to God and the universe frequently comes up in Gestalt work. I, personally, without any particular conscious intention, have moved far from my early dry and narrowly intellectual atheism as I absorbed the Gestalt style, and I have seen some of this process in others. But it has remained for Lyn Walker to explore this relation in detail, and I am delighted with how he has done it—though I am urging him in the second edition to paint and choreograph it, and set it to music.

Perhaps the most exciting feature of this book is that the myths, metaphors, and images of Christianity are not totally new, but known to me and, I suspect, to many Americans in the 1970's as a body of dead material, force-fed in Sunday school, and learned to please someone else. I never made these images alive for myself, or really went out to meet them. In Lyn Walker's discussion of "the fall," the casting out of demons, the notion of salvation as a final state, etc., these images come alive as fresh examples of the Gestalt style. The last of these examples particularly touched me at this point in my life, and I would like to expand on it as an example of the integrations this book has helped me make. I have been quite aware, in my clients and myself, of some of the secular equivalents of the delusion of permanent salvation. The businessman dreams of "having it made"; the academician more

12

genteelly seeks "tenure." The patient imagines that when he has his quota of insights, and "finishes" therapy, life will be a garden of roses. The general thinks if we win the war we will finally be safe. My particular form of the delusion was to imagine at various points in my life that I was an "expert" on something—occasionally with institutional certificates to prove it—and could therefore relax from learning anything new and difficult. Occasionally, God help me, I even think I am an expert in Gestalt therapy, and can practice the method on others without risk of involvement myself! A Gestalt principle is that the essence of the whole is re-created in each part or manifestation, so it is no surprise that a culture that leads a man to think there is permanent security on earth also offers him a heaven, in which, if he just sweats a little harder and gets there, he is welcome to stay forever without further effort. Some of the integrations I have made through Gestalt therapy have felt like bits of heaven, but each has been to itself, just for the moment, needing to be done again and again, and not even giving a guarantee that any more such integrations will follow.

PREFACE ————————————————

This book is about the relationship between religious experience and therapeutic experience. Starting with a recapitulation of the meaning of "soul" in ancient Israel, it focuses on what happens to the individual when he experiences himself as a total organism, rather than as an assemblage of unrelated parts. Repeated emphasis is given to how the self develops; how the self is disordered; and how the self is restored. Self-development, self-disorder, and self-restoration are concerns of both the religious counselor and the psychotherapist. They are concerns regarding the presence or absence of integrity, wholeness, and fulfillment in human existence. Hence, the term "religious" is used in this book to refer to strivings for, or actualizations of, integrity, wholeness, and fulfillment in self-experience rather than to focus attention on dogma and forms.

Gestalt therapy, an integrative approach to human personality and human problems, provides a useful orientation for understanding man as a psychophysical totality (the meaning of "soul" in ancient Israel) in contemporary terms. Drawing upon psychoanalysis, existential philosophy, and gestalt psychology, Gestalt therapy focuses on the total experience of the individual in the here and how. It is in the context of Gestalt therapy's holistic-organismic approach that religious experience can be conceptualized as a continual process of death and rebirth, through which the individual overcomes fragmentation, discovers and actualizes potential, and finds meaning and orientation for his existence. Moreover, the Gestalt approach frees the individual from a priori value systems, dogmas, and creeds, and orients him to the demands, values, and meanings which emerge from the here-and-now event. The aim of both Gestalt therapy and religious experience is to create conditions in which persons who are dissatisfied with the way they are may view alternative ways of being, and in which they may choose to remain as they are or to change.

Perhaps an explanation of the way Gestalt therapy works, particularly in the style of Fritz Perls, will be helpful to the reader. Gestalt therapy generally occurs in groups. Ordinarily, the therapist works with one person at a time, the primary encounter taking place between the therapist and the client. Theoretically, each group member will derive benefit from being in the group, whether he works or not, for he will identify with those features in the work of others which impinge on his own needs and problems. The group sits in a circle, with the therapist located where everyone can see him. Next to the therapist is an empty chair, called the "hot seat," where persons who want to work will sit. In front of, or near, the therapist and the hot seat is another empty chair, which is used as the imaginary location of the client's attitudes, feelings, dream-objects, significant persons, etc., and with which he will periodically carry on dialogues during his therapeutic work. For example:

16

A young man begins in the hot seat by "talking about" his mother. He is directed by the therapist to place his mother on the empty chair and "talk to" her. Having done so, he is now directed to sit on the empty chair and to answer himself as if he were his mother. As he continues to alternate between the hot seat and the empty chair, if the work is successful, the client begins to integrate his feelings (e.g., love and hate) for his mother and to complete unfinished business with her. As he is able to express his resentment toward his mother, he soon becomes aware of feelings of tenderness toward her. Further, as tenderness and resentment are integrated, he becomes capable of a relationship with his mother in which he no longer relates as a child, but as a man. More work may bring forth awareness that he has had difficult relations with women because he has tended to displace onto them resentment which he felt toward his mother.

In this process, the therapist pays attention to the client's voice, posture, gestures, facial expressions, verbal qualifications, omissions, etc., and calls the client's attention to these. Instead of offering interpretations of either verbal or non-verbal communications, the therapist instructs the client to dramatize them—to give them voices, to act them out, to paint them, to dance them, and so on—and to allow awareness of their meanings to emerge from the dramatizations. Of course, the process does not always flow smoothly. There are starts and stops; contacts and withdrawals; clarifications and confusions; progressions and impasses. Always, however, the therapist's task is to provide the adequate amounts of frustration and support that will allow the client to proceed with the work of discovering the true nature of his experience and potential.

As far as I know, this is the only book which attempts to relate the burgeoning approach of Gestalt therapy to an understanding of religious experience. I hope the book will be meaningful to therapists who are interested in the humanistic-existential emphases of contemporary psychotherapy, to psychologists of religion, to pastoral counselors, to clergymen, to students, and to "seekers" who are interested in understanding, and creating conditions for, the development of whole persons. In any case, I hope the book will suggest new ways of viewing both religious and therapeutic experience.

Several persons have helped me to write this book, both directly and indirectly. I am grateful to my friend Willis E. Wygant, Chaplain-Supervisor at San Mateo County General Hospital, for introducing me to Gestalt therapy in 1967; to Jack Downing and Cynthia Werthman of the San Francisco Gestalt Institute, for helping me to understand both the theory and practice of Gestalt therapy in the first phase of my continuing training program; to Robert C. Leslie, Edward V. Stein, Aaron J. Ungersma, Paul W. Morentz, teachers, friends, and now colleagues, who helped in the development of this book at various stages with criticisms, suggestions, and support; to Roy Fairchild, teacher, friend, and colleague, whose help was invaluable and whose Foreword is precious; to John Enright of the San Francisco Gestalt Institute, who, without always being aware of it, has taught me a great deal, has made helpful suggestions for this book, and has written a stimulating Foreword; and finally to my friend Arthur L. Foster, now at Chicago Theological Seminary, who first suggested that I write this book.

Diane Gilkerson diligently typed this manuscript through several versions, patiently tolerating my confused and confusing directions and my last-minute changes. Mrs. Joseph (Billie) Elliott put in extra time at the Graduate Theological Union in order to type final revisions for publication. I also want to express my gratitude to Hubert S. Coffey, my advisor in the Psychology Department, University of California at

Berkeley, who guided me through the maze that is the University during my studies there. Finally, I am grateful to my friend Sheila Fabricant for preparing the index.

While I am grateful to many persons for contributing to the strengths of this book, I am aware of some of its limitations and weaknesses, for which I alone am responsible.

CONTENTS

I
BODY
AND
SOUL

Whatever one says about the human soul—if it hits the mark at all—will be both right and wrong. Psychological material is so complex that every statement is inadequate. We can no more stand back from the psyche and look at it objectively than we can get away from ourselves. If we are anything we are psyche. —James Hillman, *Suicide and the Soul*

Then the Lord God formed man of dust from the ground, and breathed into his nostrils the breath of life; and man became a living being.— Genesis 2:7 RSV

Modern man needs an understanding of the human self which is neither purely psychologistic nor purely naturalistic, yet which integrates the wisdom of both psychology and naturalism. I think that such a conception existed in ancient Israel's understanding of man, and is now being worked out in contemporary language in Gestalt therapy, an exciting theoretical and therapeutic approach to human existence.

Though the word "crisis" is currently bandied about, the modern crisis of human existence is very real, whether we think of existence in the sense of physical survival or in the sense of meaningful living. The ambiguity of modern existence is most apparent in strong desires for peace in the face of improvements in the technology of war; in attempts to limit the testing and use of nuclear weapons and the simultaneous development of bigger and "better" bombs; in progressive elimination of the drudgery of physical activity and escalation of the pollution of the physical environment; in the tension between the concerns for physical ecology and the

23

problems in human ecology; in increasing capacities to extend the quantity of life and increasing difficulties in promoting the quality of life. We have become "civilized" at the awful expense of the denial of essential aspects of human nature, and in the process we have developed (out of an alleged sophistication that increasingly reveals itself as mere sophistry) the means whereby we may destroy ourselves. Furthermore, in testimony to an apparent compulsion to destroy everything we touch, a scientist has suggested that since we have studied the moon's surface rocks and soil, we now should explode a bomb on the farther side of the moon in order to study the moon's internal composition. Although we are capable, perhaps as never before in human history, of creating the conditions which will allow for the unfolding of hitherto undiscovered human potentialities, we are also capable of more complete human degradation and destruction than ever before. In short, we are engaged in a critical life-and-death struggle. In a real sense, we must *choose* between life and death, and the outcome is uncertain not only because of the complexities of modern existence, but also because of our indecisiveness in making choices and taking reasonable risks. We cannot avoid the fact that, in the final analysis, we shape our existence by the choices we make (even if we choose to allow someone else to make choices for us). Therefore, the human being is unable to escape responsibility for his existence, for, as Naranjo maintains: "At depth, we are where we want to be, we are doing what we want to do, even when it amounts to apparent tragedy." [1]

Modern human existence is characterized by superficiality, alienation, fragmentation, and estrangement which are based upon our denial of essential aspects of human nature. However, our increasing awareness of the critical nature of our

[1] Joen Fagan and Irma Shepherd, eds., *Gestalt Therapy Now* (Palo Alto, Calif.: Science and Behavior Books, 1970), p. 68.

24

individual, interpersonal, and international situation is calling our attention to our extremely limited understanding of what it means to be human. Particularly in Western civilization, where technology dominates, critics assert that we have been so dehumanized that, except in emergency situations wherein conditioned responses collapse and spontaneity results, we ordinarily use only 10 to 25 percent of our potential. Whether or not the percentages are accurate, the fact is that we do not know the limits of the farther reaches of human awareness and potential. Yet, perhaps for the first time in human history, we are learning how to establish the conditions in which these outer limits might be explored. (See Appendix A.)

Wilson Van Dusen points out that "the term *existential* has come to be nearly equivalent to the term *critical*." [2] It is not surprising, therefore, that in the context of our current crisis of existence, existential-humanistic-phenomenological emphases are becoming predominant both in the theoretical and in the practical areas of life. Our conviction is growing that modern man's salvation, if it is to become a reality, is contingent upon rediscovery of total existence, upon restoration of those essential aspects of human nature which we have both avoided and denigrated, and upon overcoming the alienation, fragmentation, and estrangement of which we are both creators and victims. However, this rediscovery of total existence is, in turn, contingent upon a radical overhauling of the conception of man which prevails in Western civilization. The popular interpretation of the "original sin" conception has it that man, the animated Humpty-Dumpty, was irreparably split by his "fall" into various unalterably opposed fragments which are incapable of integration. This awful notion of *massa perditionis* implies that the greatest hope is that man will be adjustable to some generally agreeable or

---

[2] Wilson Van Dusen, "Existential Analytic Psychotherapy," *American Journal of Psychoanalysis*, XX (1960), 37.

"normal" pattern. In contrast, the existential-humanistic-phenomenological emphases focus on the phenomenal existence of individuals, as they wrestle with the polarities and ambiguities of their existence and attempt thereby to shape the meaning of their self-experience. In other words, the focus is on the choices which the individual makes and avoids in the continually unfolding critical moments of his life. Through this focus, we discover the potentialities of human experience which remain hidden when our scrutiny of self-experience is based upon prior conceptions, to which we try to fit human experience.

Our prevailing understanding of human nature is largely dualistic. For various reasons, we deal with such dichotomies as mind and body, soul and body, and spirit and matter as if we are referring to completely separate and autonomous entities. Consequently, persons have been encouraged, where not required, to subdue, deny, and ignore the body and to pursue vaguely defined "higher" goals. (We even tend to speak of lower and higher brain centers with valuational implications.) As I shall show, the tendency to conceive of such dichotomies as body and soul as referring to separate and autonomous entities merely contributes to the truncation of human experience. The body is the mediator of the human experience of reality, and alienation of the body cuts one off from reality. One cannot avoid his body, through which all sensations, perceptions, emotions, ideas, and images are mediated exclusively, without experiencing distortion—hence disorder—in the psyche. Separation from the body results in the elaboration of imagery which is not connected with actuality. Man's alienation, fragmentation, and estrangement mean, then, that one who denies his body and who therefore does not know what he feels, senses, perceives—in a word, experiences—also cannot know who he is. Hence, since he feels like a stranger to himself, he is incapable of encountering others in any authentic way. We know now that true selfhood is based upon the awareness of instinctual [3] and biological urges which we learn, ideally in early childhood, to recognize and to accept as our own and to fulfill with intentional deliberateness. It follows that our human experience is truncated to the extent that we learn to deny the biological and instinctual base of our existence, for in this denial we run the risk either of becoming lifeless robots, or of being overwhelmed and controlled by unaware organismic strivings. In either case, we take no responsibility for our existence. We need then to overcome the avoidance of experience, not through adjustment, but through the re-centering of our lives in the integration of body and soul.

Rollo May, in a series of articles entitled "Religion, Psychotherapy, and the Achievement of Selfhood," raised the question of the relation between the capacity for affirming one's own being and the historical and psychological meaning of the term soul. He wrote:

> As I understand it, the concept of man's soul has meant through history that center of the human being's self-awareness in which inhered his capacity for self-direction, ultimate choices and responsibility; the center in which his decisions transcended time and space in that they dealt with his ultimate concerns; that center of self-awareness which distinguished the human beings from animals and the rest of nature. [4]

May asserts that the reification of soul, in such phrases as "man *has* a soul," and the use of soul in the Cartesian sense

---

[3] If we remember that we are dealing with the human being, who is defined by the capacity to make choices and decisions, to utilize his awareness with intentional deliberateness, we need not discard the term "instinctual." This term implies the automatic or innate quality of certain urges, needs, drives, sensations, etc., which the *human* being can *choose* to fulfill or gratify (or delay) through his ingenious capacity to symbolize, and so on.

[4] *Pastoral Psychology*, November 1951, p. 20.

of an entity residing in the pineal gland where mind and body were connected led to scientific rejection of the concept as a source of intellectual laziness and dishonesty. However, pointing out that Freud and the European analysts used the term psyche literally, and were therefore closer to the truth than "scientific" psychologists who favor the constrictive forms of mathematical and atomistic research, May feels that both psychological and religious thinkers can assume that there must be some classical, operational truth embodied in the concept of soul for it to have persisted so long in history. (See Appendix B for Hillman's summary of the historical and contemporary meanings of the root metaphor of psychology, namely, the psyche or soul.)

I contend that we are now aided in the explication of "the classical, operational truth" of the concept "soul" by delineating the meaning and message of Gestalt therapy, in which *the center of the personality,* namely, the emotions, the feelings, the spirit, constitutes what used to be called the soul. However, I want to set the context for my consideration of the relevance of Gestalt therapy—which in both theory and practice starts and ends with a holistic view of man—by recapitulating the naturalistic and holistic understanding of man which is our heritage from ancient Israel.

Body and Soul

I suggested earlier that we need a radical overhauling of our understanding of man. The term "overhaul" implies an examination leading to necessary adjustments and repairs which will restore something (e.g., a motor) to good working order. Hence, in the case of overhauling a car's motor, the owner will not have to purchase a new motor, but will pay only for necessary adjustments and repairs. The analogy holds for what I am about in overhauling our understanding of man. Much that we feel, think, and know about human nature is valid. However, throughout history various emphases have predominated which have thrown human beings out of balance, and certain adjustments and realignments are now required if we are to recover "the classical, operational truth embodied in the concept of soul." I think that the clearest explication of this classical, operational truth in antiquity is to be found in the life and culture of ancient Israel.

Ancient Israel's understanding of man is succinctly summarized in the creation myth of Genesis, chapters 1 and 2. This biblical myth, commonly called the second creation story because it follows the myth in chapter 1, is actually the older story in regards to composition date. Of course, the story in Genesis 1 seems to receive greater attention when the interest is in expounding a positive doctrine of man. This is particularly noteworthy in light of the cosmic emphasis of Genesis 1, in contrast to the man-earth emphasis of Genesis 2. (Hereafter Genesis 2 will be shorthand for the creation narrative which is actually contained in Genesis 2 and 3.) The avoidance of Genesis 2 in Judeo-Christian culture could well betray a resistance to its implications, which contradict the prevailing dichotomies—such as mind and body—of our culture. Generally, an underlying assumption seems to be that when one is interested in providing a religious basis for the understanding of man's essential nature, he should focus on the *imago Dei* passage of Genesis 1; and when one is interested in explicating the meaning of man's violation of the *imago Dei,* he should focus on Genesis 2. I do not wish to argue the relative merits of these two creation myths. Here I simply want to make the point that even the most sophisticated of us are inclined to betray our discomfiture with the man-earth emphasis of Genesis 2 by avoiding it.

Genesis 2 is clear about man's wholeness and unity. It

clearly and directly depicts man as a psycho-physical totality or self. The objection might be raised that if man is a totality of soul (*psyche*) and body (*physike; physikos*), the hyphenation of psycho-physical implies that they are separate and distinct entities. On the contrary, the hyphenation here merely affirms the *possibility* of the mind-body or soul-body split in human experience. Or, as Hillman puts it, "It is this question—what have the body and soul to do with each other—that the soul is continually putting to us in philosophy, religion, art, and above all in the trials of daily life and death."[5] In the sense, then, that each of us is continually torn between the claims of body and soul, each of us is split. Another way to say this is that there is a continual struggle between body and soul for exclusive control of human existence. We all know persons who, obsessed with fulfilling instinctual and biological urges (gustatory, tactual, sexual, and so on), constrict life-energy to one sphere of life so that, for instance, all of life may be sexualized, or gustatory greed may be transferred to every realm of existence.

In verse 7 of Genesis 2, the word *nephesh* is used to denote the whole person: "Then the Lord God formed man of dust from the ground, and breathed into his nostrils the breath of life; and man became a living *nephesh*." Nephesh is rendered as "soul" in the King James Version and as "being" in the Revised Standard Version. In a paper on Hebrew psychology, H. Wheeler Robinson points out that there is no reason to doubt that the primary meaning of *nephesh* was breath. He writes:

One of the most widely spread ideas of general anthropology is to identify the life-principle, and ultimately all the phenomena of consciousness, with the breath, for while there is breath there is life. But in Hebrew usage another word (*neshamah*) came to denote "breath," and *nephesh* was reserved for . . . psychical

[5] *Suicide and the Soul* (New York: Harper & Row, 1964), p. 46.

30

uses, . . . though always with the thought of "breath" as the life-principle, underlying the usage. This breath-soul is conceived as the animating principle of man's life, its essential constituent, though as much dependent on bodily organs for its activity as these are dependent on it for life itself. This virtual identification with the breath shows that the "soul" is quasi-materialistically conceived.[6]

Moreover, Robinson points out that ancient Hebrew culture attributed psychical functions to parts of the body which to us seem to be purely physiological. In ancient Hebrew culture the phrase "body and soul" gave an exhaustive description of human personality—a notion that is difficult for us to grasp, influenced as we have been by the dichotomies of Greek and modern psychology. Any one of the body parts could be regarded by the ancient Hebrews as a center of consciousness, since the psychical and physical (physiological) were not distinguished. Hence,

> If then we ask again the old question, "What is man?" and try to answer it, not in the old theological, but in the new psychological fashion, we shall say that for the Hebrew, man is a unity, and that that unity is the body as a complex of parts, drawing their life and activity from a breath-soul, which has no existence apart from the body.[7]

While it might be contended that *nephesh* is free of the vagueness and ambiguity which attaches to the *imago Dei* notion of chapter 1, it should be noted that in ancient thought the word for image was not constricted to man's spiritual nature, but also applied to his whole being, including the body, which the ancients considered a divine work of art. Properly used, then, the Hebrew word for image refers to very concrete, visible things, or at least to things which have meaningful referents. For example, an image of the king, left

[6] Arthur S. Peake, *The People and the Book* (Oxford: Clarendon Press, 1925), pp. 356-57.
[7] *Ibid.*, p. 366.

31

behind in one of his provinces, represented the king's actual authority. Likewise, man, created in the image of God, is God's representative in the cosmos and, more particularly, in the earth. Therefore, even Genesis 1 implies man's totality of body and soul. However, I choose here to concentrate on Genesis 2 because, in contrast to the primary interest in Genesis 1 in the cosmos or the entire universe, Genesis 2 is concerned with the much narrower and more immediate realm of the earth. Indeed, the primary theme of Genesis 2 is *'adam-'adama* (man-earth), the ecological unity of man and his environment. It is therefore appropriate to speak of man as being in the earth, rather than on it, in acknowledgement of the intimate bond between man and his environment (including humankind). In this narrative the universe is regarded quite anthropocentrically, for the focus is on man and the world of man's life. In Genesis 1, the emphasis is reversed: man is regarded quite cosmically. In the anthropocentric emphasis of Genesis 2, the plants and the animals are established around man. Man is the primary creature, and all that comes before man's creation merely sets the context for the first action of the narrative, namely, the creation of man. The bond of life between man (*'adam*) and earth or ground (*'adama*) is firmly fixed in man's formation from dust from the ground.

However, though man derives his corporeal substance from the ground, he becomes a living creature only when the Creator's breath is united with his body. The material body, a mere fragile substance, is enlivened by the inspiration of the Creator's life-giving breath, and the implication is that the proper distinction is between body and life, rather than between body and soul, for soul is the energy that characterizes life. Stated differently, man's "soul-fulness" is his quality of liveliness, vitality, and power, without which he is a mere lifeless body, a mummy or robot. Just as man, before receiv-

32

ing breath is a lifeless body, he will revert, when breath is gone, to lifelessness and ultimate decay. Again, Wheeler Robinson points out that Hebrew has no proper word for body as separate from soul.

> It never needed one so long as the body was the man; definition and nomenclature come in only when there is some conscious antithesis. That antithesis is not reached in the Old Testament, nor could it be reached along native lines of Hebrew thought.[8]

This organismic or holistic conception of man earns for verse 7 of Genesis 2 the label of the *locus classicus* of Old Testament anthropology.

Man as Grounded and Earthy

It is important to note that the explicit intimate bond between man and the earth in this narrative is not intended to degrade man in any sense. Instead, the bond conveys the reality of man as a grounded creature, existing in a relationship of interdependence with his environment. Moreover, man is grounded, centered down, in the sense that earthiness is an essential aspect of his being, no less important than other aspects. We are aware of this, for we often use the term "earthy" to indicate that a person is in contact with his roots, is reality-oriented, is in touch with his body, through which he experiences and molds reality. We say of the earthy person that he "has his feet on the ground," or he "is a solid person." He has a sense of involvement (in the sense of participation) in life's realities and is, therefore, as serious about the mundane and commonplace as about the transcendent and extraordinary. Indeed, for the earthy person such dichotomies are basically insignificant. On the other hand, we speak of a person who is out of touch with his roots, who is not grounded in reality, as aloof, up in the air, moonstruck,

[8] *Ibid.*

33

a lunatic, and so on (though recent moon explorations may require changes in our imagery). The person who frowns upon earthiness usually is shallow, and this shallowness might be expressed through his inability to be *alone with himself* (when he is physically alone, he still avoids his self-experience); through his continual search for *the* fulfilling friendship, marriage, love affair, or esthetic experience; or through his incomplete presence in life's ongoing process and a consequent dissatisfaction with what *is*. The projection or alienation of earthiness inevitably results in endless operations to shore up an image that will fill the void. In our culture, many allegedly cultured persons merely exist in "things" (music, art, literature) because they do not feel at home in their bodies, whereas for the grounded, centered, earthy person these artifacts are extensions of the self.

Insofar as the emphasis in Genesis 2 is on man *and* earth (or "man-earth"), everything occurs in a very earthy and earthly way. Man, formed out of the womb of mother earth, is of a piece with the earth. He receives his body from the *blessed* earth, for it is only after the fall that the earth is "cursed" by the Creator and man is "condemned" to eke out a living from this cursed ground. Therefore, the intimate bond between man and the earth is affirmed even in the fact that man's action has consequences for the earth's wellbeing.[9] More importantly, the narrative at no point even implies that the body is man's prison, or shell, or *mere exterior*; rather, the body is man himself. Dietrich Bonhoeffer explains it as follows:

* The animism of ancient (or primitive) culture can be understood only when seen in the context of the synthesis of man and nature which the "primitives" recognized and appreciated. Though our scientific discoveries have freed us from some of the simplistic conclusions of primitive culture, we need to recover the awareness that man as *homo sapiens* does not cease to be an animal, a creature, intricately and intimately bound up with nature.

34

Man does not "have" a body; he does not "have" a soul; rather he "is" body and soul. Man in the beginning is really his body. He is one. . . . The man who renounces his body renounces his existence before God the Creator. The essential point of human existence is its bond with mother earth, its being as body. Man has his existence as existence on earth; he does not come to the earthly world from above, driven and enslaved by a cruel fate. He comes out of the earth.[10]

Groundedness or earthiness represents, then, man's unity within himself and with his environment, animate and inanimate, and the grounded body is the center of man's existence as an inspirited creature. In other words, in man's bodiliness he is related to the earth and to others; he is there for others, for he is mediated to the world and the world is mediated to him exclusively through the body.

Since it is the breath (spirit) of the Creator which makes the body live, to live as man means to live as body and spirit. Again, Bonhoeffer writes: "Escape from the body is escape from being man and escape from the spirit as well. Body is the existence-form of spirit, as spirit is the existence-form of body." [11] In short, body and spirit form an inseparable unity. Therefore, we cannot speak accurately of inferior aspects of human nature, for man is a totality who can be wholly understood only when understood as a whole. The Creator forms creatures who come to life only through *inspiration*. Moreover, man the creature is, in turn, able to create and to give life to his world. Through this creative capacity, man the creature expresses his likeness to the Creator and thereby realizes the *imago Dei*, or personality potential, which is embedded in his nature. Stated differently, the Creator forms creatures, not tools, who are capable of participating in a continuing process of creation and creativity, in which process

[10] *Creation and Fall*, trans. John C. Fletcher (New York: The Macmillan Co., 1959), pp. 46-47.
[11] *Ibid.*, p. 47.

35

the creatures re-create and renew themselves and their world again and again.[12]

It should be apparent by now that the narrator of this myth is not interested in mere abstractions which cannot be related to actuality. Since it is older than the myth of Genesis 1, perhaps this narrative is truer to the life and culture of ancient Israel, which seem to have taken phenomenal reality seriously in every respect. The peculiar double-talk of Judeo-Christian culture which both affirms and disaffirms the goodness of creation, that is, of material reality, is missing in the culture of ancient Israel. At no point does the narrator of the myth qualify his characterization of man as a peculiar totality of body and soul.

The Parts and the Whole

In order to understand the conception of man as a soul in his total essence, rather than as a body supplied with a soul, we need to understand the meaning(s) of the word *nephesh* (soul; being) as it was used in the life and culture of ancient Israel.[13] In contrast to our prevailing sharply defined dimensions of body and soul, the Israelitic view was of a relation of complete unification between body and soul in which soul means, first and foremost, a totality with a peculiar stamp. They did not conceive of a mind-body duality, but of a unification or integration of all aspects of human nature into a whole. Furthermore, in the Israelitic view, man does not differ in this respect from other forms of life, for the other creatures (beasts of the field and birds of the air) are also formed from the ground, and, according to Pedersen, "if we

[12] The reader is urged to consult *The Oxford English Dictionary*, Volume II, for a provocative study of the etymological relationships of the words "creator," "creature," and "creative."
[13] In this section, I am indebted to Johannes Pedersen for his intensive analysis of the word *nephesh* in *Israel: Its Life and Culture* (London: Oxford University Press, 1926) II, 98-181.

read the priestly account of the creation [i.e., Genesis 1], we learn that it is not only man who is a soul, but also the animals. The animal world in its various genera consists of mere souls. It is a swarm of living souls who fill the earth." [14] In short, man and other living creatures are animated souls.

As a soul, man cannot desist from being a connected whole, a *characteristic unity of volition or intentionality and act*. In ancient Israel, therefore, there is no independent term for will as we know it. Instead, man as soul is penetrated entirely by his sensations (perceptions, urges, needs, "instincts"). The whole tendency or intention of a man, based on the sensations which penetrate his being, is what constitutes the will. It follows that ancient Israel had no separate categories for objective and subjective thinking. All *thinking* had implications for direct, immediate action, and there was no such thing as inactive, theoretical thinking without such implications. (Compare with this conception Heisenberg's principle that in the very act of observing a phenomenon we change it, and you can begin to get a sense of what the Israelites meant.) Logic, then, consists of immediate perception, rather than empty abstraction. Even memory is connected with action and actuality, and the Israelitic word *zakhar* which means "to remember, to call to mind, to commemorate" also means "to begin an action, to proceed to do something." (This *active commemoration* is maintained in the New Testament by Jesus the Jew, who commanded his disciples at the Last Supper to commemorate his life, and their life together, by breaking bread and drinking wine [participatory acts], thereby implying that mere words are inadequate for authentic, fulfilling commemoration or remembrance. In such active commemoration, proprioceptive awareness is added to one's experience, making it more complete than it would be if one

[14] *Ibid.*, p. 100.

37

were inactive. Of course, yoga and isometric exercises teach us that "activity" or "e-motion" need not be obvious to be authentic.) The point is that in ancient Israel the term for memory takes for granted an effect on the total self and its direction of will.

Moreover, in ancient Israel, expression was intimately involved with the soul, or rather reflective *of* the soul. "The word is the form of vesture of the contents of the soul, its bodily expression." [15] To claim, therefore, that communication problems were mere matters of semantics was foreign to the ancient Israelite. Confused communication, to them, would be an expression of the confused state of one's soul. By the same token, powerful communication would be an expression of the power of the soul, and it is no wonder that in ancient Israel actual death could be made to occur by *speaking*. In fact, *we* sometimes say that a person was "killed" by the words of another, indicating awareness at some level of the potential embodiment of one's totality, hence power, in his words. In addition, the physical body is the soul in its outward form. Bodily sensations are felt through the entirety of the soul, and the bowels and the belly are identified with the soul. Psychosomatic medicine has revealed to us the participation of bowels and belly in emotional or psychical experience, whether we inhibit emotion, and thereby cause ulcers, ulcerative colitis, and so on, or whether we express emotion strongly, as in rage, when adrenalin production increases. In practically every culture deep emotions are referred to in terms of bowels and belly, as in our phrase "gut-level reaction or feeling." In Greek, for example, the word which means "to move one's bowels" also means "to have compassion." Further, the Israelites saw the soul as prominent in the head, and particularly in the face and its expression. We also have a growing faith in our ability to "read" a person's

[15] *Ibid.*

attitudes from his posture, gestures, facial expressions, or motility, along with a growing suspicion of verbalization, because in our culture words tend to be used as much to obscure as to express experience.

The breath is the soul, the animating, vital principle of life. The Israelites consistently maintained that the breath is the soul entirely. In other words, breath is the power that creates and sustains life; it is the energy of life. The breath thinks: "The spirit of man is the lamp of the Lord, searching all his innermost parts." The King James Version is more explicit: "The *spirit* of man *is* the candle of Yahweh *searching all the inward parts of the belly*" (Prov. 20:27). Recent therapeutic discoveries or innovations, especially those of a Reichian bent, point out that shallow breathing, that is breathing that is not abdominal, has its counterparts, in the emotional-psychological sphere, in "shallow" thinking, feeling, and acting (hence, the italics in the above-quoted passage). The breath is the wise, acting soul which makes good counsel: "With whose help have you uttered words, and whose spirit has come forth from you?" Again the King James Version is more direct: "To whom hast thou uttered words? and whose *spirit* came from thee?" (Job 26:4). The breath of God gives life: "The spirit of God has made me, and the *breath* of the Almighty gives me life" (Job 33:4; cf. Gen. 2:7). It is important to note that the terms "soul," "spirit," and "breath" are interchangeable in the life and thought of ancient Israel and that they are valid translations of the same word. Thus when the narrator of the creation myth speaks of the Creator's breathing into man's nostrils the breath of life, he is neither playing with words, nor being ostentatious. Man becomes a living spirit; a living breath; a living soul. It may just as well be said that God created breath as that he created spirits or souls. In fact, Pedersen observes that the last verse of the book of Psalms reads: "Let every thing that hath breath praise

39

Yahweh." This is the King James Version. The Revised
Standard Version says: 'Let everything that breathes praise
the Lord!" (Ps. 150:6).

Etymologically the word "spirit" is related to such words
as animation, vitality, excitement, excitability, and so on. The
root meaning of spirit, which derives from *spirare*, is "to
breathe; breathing; breath." Derivative meanings and/or implications include capacity, potential, power, influence, creativity, essence, energy, and inspiration. All these words refer
to aliveness or to qualities of aliveness, and reference to them
illuminates the Israelites' contention that spirit is life. It is
spirit which infuses the bodily substance with liveliness and
which makes possible the actualization of the peculiarly human potentialities (self-awareness, imagination, and symbolization) which distinguish man from the other creatures. I
have pointed out the Israelitic view that all creatures, including man, are souls, and that man is a soul with a "peculiar
stamp." In contemporary terms, we can now explain man's
peculiar stamp. So far as we know, man is the only creature
whose twofold dominant trait is awareness of himself as a
unique individual (or rather the capacity for this awareness)
and awareness of his potential nonbeing or death. Included
in this awareness is the capacity for self-transcendence, which
allows man to re-form or re-shape himself through a synthesis
of memory, actuality, and anticipation.

Life and Death

We get from ancient Israel not only an understanding of
life, but also an understanding of death, based on the holistic
understanding of man. In ancient Israel, life and death are
not two sharply distinguished spheres having to do with
existence and nonexistence, as we understand them. Rather,
life is for them something which one possesses in a higher or

lower degree. Therefore, death cannot strike a part of the self, whether in the physiological or psychological sphere, without affecting the totality of the self. When the body or any other part of the soul is diseased or damaged, the entire personality is affected. There is, in this conception, a sense of the acceptance of the eventuality of actual death which encourages individuals to grapple as completely as possible with the issues of daily life and death. In other words, out of full awareness of the eventuality of actual death, one eschews death-in-life and vigorously attempts to fulfill the potentialities of each present moment. The ancient Israelites were true existentialists, then, in the sense that they considered every moment of existence a critical moment. For them, the soul was at every moment expressing the measure of its participation in life or of its withdrawal into death. Hence, it was very meaningful to them when the sick person or one otherwise in distress spoke of himself as dead, and upon recovery, of being pulled out of death, returned to life. In the understanding of ancient Israel, "illness is death, healing life," [16] and in this understanding one can speak as meaningfully of the sick soul as of the sick body.

In this context I want to say something about "spirituality," which we tend to use as a mere abstraction, unrelated to actuality and referring to some nether world. If we follow the holistic conception of ancient Israel, spirituality means liveliness, vitality, creativity, excitement, excitability, and so on, and stagnation, emptiness, sterility, and deadness represent constricted or inhibited spirituality. The issue of spirituality is, then, a mater of life and death, or, more clearly, of aliveness and deadness. The needful thing, if we would recover spirituality, which has been "abstracted" from actuality, is recovery of the body, the center of existence, and hence the recovery

[16] *Ibid.*, p. 167.

41

of the life-energy, of the breath-soul. When one recovers or re-owns his body, he experiences the only kind of revival that is authentic, namely, revival in the sense of *revivere,* "to live again." When one who has avoided essential aspects of his experience brings the self back into attention, being, and use as a totality, rather than as an assembly of varied and sundry separate parts, he again is able to participate in life's ongoing process of change and growth. He realizes the full import of the truism that with man "the whole is greater than the sum of its parts."

In light of this holistic conception, we can see life-and-death, death-and-rebirth imagery as perhaps the most adequate imagery for describing the problematic existence of modern man and prescribing remedies for it. The paradox of modern life is that the more loudly we affirm life, the more furiously we create the conditions for death. Moreover, we deny or avoid the reality of death in many ways[17] and think thereby that we are able to participate more fully in life, whereas Hillman asserts that "until we can *choose* death, we cannot *choose* life." [18] In order to understand this, we must understand how the dualistic distortion of man that prevails in our culture contributes to our deadness, for it is under this dualism that the holistic-naturalistic conception of man, which is our heritage from ancient Israel, is buried.

---

[17] See Jessica Mitford, *The American Way of Death* (New York: Simon and Schuster, 1963), which more than adequately documents how the funeral industry thrives on the denial of death in our culture.

[18] *Suicide and the Soul,* p. 63; emphasis mine.

II
TOTALITY
AND
REALITY

The question arises whether integration and wholeness
equal salvation, to which the response can be only that the
total self is involved in one's experience, whether that experience be of salvation or degradation. The basis of our
difficulty in accepting and understanding this notion is the
dualism which pervades our culture. Moreover, we conceive
of salvation as a state which, at some point and through
proper procedures, can be achieved and finalized. These are
spurious notions that persist because the Hebraic notion of
man as a psychophysical self has been overshadowed by Hellenistic dualism, which considers the realm of matter illusory
or evil and prefers a vaguely defined "spiritual" realm. On
the basis of such a dualistic conception, it is possible to think
that no matter how terrible life may appear, there is a realm
in which everything is all right. This dualism, which overwhelmed the Judeo-Christian religion in the early centuries

of its history, has been and is a tenacious influence in this culture. Based on its influence, the Judeo-Christian religion inaugurated a split between body and soul which resulted in denigration, if not outright condemnation, of the body. As a carrier of the instincts, the body was labeled despicable and sinful. Consequently, the following statement by Perls, though a caricature, is hard to refute without a significant measure of defensiveness:

> If you are a Christian, you should be unsubstantial. In the New Testament nature doesn't count: only the supernatural, miraculous counts. And if you are dead, you should not be dead. Everything is regarded as if it should not exist as it is. In other words, the constitution with which we are born—our inheritance—is despised. We are not allowed to be at home in ourselves, so we alienate those frowned-upon properties and create the holes, . . . the nothingness where something should exist. And where there is something missing, we build up a phony artifact.[1]

Granted, Perls is expounding a position which is relevant to the explicit and implicit ambiguities and distortions in the thinking of Paul rather than to the thinking of Jesus. Nevertheless, it is true that followers of the Judeo-Christian religion are not easily convinced of the correctness of holistic thinking. Generally we take for granted the theory that mind and body, or soul and body, are two different things joined together.

It is difficult, therefore, for us to recover the positive attitude toward life which does not ignore the inevitability of ambiguity, conflict, tension, frustration; in a word, evil. Yet, it is the positive, faithful attitude that is our authentic heritage from ancient Israel. We tend to sneer at the naturalistic perspective and to avoid seeing it as an expression of an accepting and essential attitude toward the physical, material realm of existence. Moreover, we tend to separate ourselves from na-

[1] Fagan and Shepherd, *Gestalt Therapy Now*, pp. 20-21.

ture and to rationalize that a "higher" nature in ourselves justifies this separation. Yet, when we are asked to define this higher nature, we are generally unable to say what it is or what it means. We only know that we sound good when we talk this way. Consequently, we consider nature as something that exists for our use, rather than as something which can and does exist in its own right, and yet to which we are intricately bound and related. This anti-naturalistic attitude results in a peculiar kind of double-talk in Judeo-Christian culture. On the one hand, the Judeo-Christian religion affirms the goodness of the created order, and even asserts that the incarnation and embodiment of God took place in Jesus the Christ as the central event of history and as confirmation of the goodness of the physical, material realm. On the other hand, the goodness of the physical, material realm is qualified so strongly that naturalism and supernaturalism are seen ultimately as diametrically and unalterably opposed. The real problem seems to be that the concern with supernaturalism derives from our denial, rather than our acceptance and fulfillment, of naturalism. Therefore, Judeo-Christian culture tends to assume a strangely "paternalistic" attitude toward the Creator, thereby betraying a faithlessness regarding the supernatural realm with which the culture is preoccupied. (Notice the number of laws, religious and political, which have been passed to protect "the sacred.")

While it is wise to be wary of human*ism* and natural*ism*, it is at the same time necessary to recognize that the natural and the human are inseparable. Therefore, the avoidance of the naturalistic and the humanistic perspectives merely guarantees the distortion of human existence. The current ecological crisis in both the physical and human spheres, for example, is merely one expression of the dangers inherent in spurious dichotomies which denigrate essential realms of existence. The fact is that in the human sphere we are as much like each other as we are different. In the physical or natural realm, we are as much a part of nature as we are separate from it.

The Dualistic Distortion of Man

In his book *Sex in Christianity and Psychoanalysis*, William Graham Cole, in something of an apology for Christianity, contends that the dualistic strand as a dominant pattern in Western civilization is a contribution of Hellenistic culture which began in the fourth century B.C. Further, he contends, Hellenistic culture was influenced by Oriental mystery cults which blended with their Hellenistic counterparts. Even Judaism, with its naturalistic heritage from patriarch and prophet, was affected by dualism in the Persian and Greek periods of Israel's history.[2] Charles B. Ketcham gives the following reasons why Christianity, though emerging from Judaism, became so characteristically Greek: First, Christianity's great growth, following its beginning in Jerusalem, was in the gentile communities of the Mediterranean world. Second, Christianity began at a time when Judaism was being profoundly influenced by Philo, the Jewish Hellenistic philosopher. Third, and most important, Christianity had to make its way in a culture dominated by Greek thought.[3] Ketcham goes on to contend that the great Church councils of early Christian history were basically defensive in nature, rather than confessional. They met for the purpose of defending the Church against the attacks, and what it perceived to be the misrepresentations, which derived from Greek intellectualism. The resulting creeds were intended,

[2] (New York: Oxford University Press, 1955), p. 3.
[3] *The Search for Meaningful Existence* (New York: Weybright and Talley, 1968), pp. 77-78.

then, more as translations of limitations to guide Greek philosophical inquiry into the nature of Christian belief than as articles of faith. The councils were designed to neutralize the antagonistic Greek philosophy, and they attempted to discharge their tasks by explaining Christian belief in the language of the enemy. The inadvertent result was that preoccupation with Greek metaphysical forms became the primary focus in Western theological thought, and Jewish mysticism and monotheism were lost—irretrievably, it seems—in Greek logic and metaphysics. Almost invariably, whenever an individual or group assumes a basically negative or defensive stance, the result is either indecisiveness or apparent loss of all connection with the original position, without enrichment having occurred in the process. So it was with Christianity in the face of Hellenistic thought. Cole contends that the most obvious victory of Greek dualism over our heritage of naturalism and holism from Hebraic thought is in the realm of sex. This victory of dualism has resulted in what might be called "schizoid sex," that is, sexual relations in which there is a split in the self and in which there is lacking a sense of total participation. It is as if the individual at one and the same time participates in the sexual relationship and stands off to observe his performance. One very clear expression of this victory of Hellenistic dualism in our culture is the proliferation of "sex manuals" which are designed to help the individual improve his performance, though striving for the technically perfect performance is a sure guarantee of robbing this spontaneous, ecstatic experience of its life. However, while the victory of dualism is most obvious in the realm of sex in our culture, we are learning—and accepting more and more—the fact that the body is the exclusive medium of our experience of the world. In behavioristic language, stimuli are mediated through the organism before the response is made (S-O-R).[4] Therefore, we are becoming aware of the awesome burdens which derive from dualism in all spheres of our existence, not just the sexual sphere.

Paul, the great systematizer of early Christianity, played a very large part in the conquest of the Judeo-Christian religion by the Hellenistic-Oriental dualism. Whereas the emphasis of ancient Israel and of Jesus the Jew called for inward integrity, for wholeness, and for unity of emotion and act, the emphasis of Paul, the Hellenized Pharisee, strongly embraced the Law, which called for outward conformity to legalism and moralism, which Cole calls the forerunners of prudery. This is the tension between Gospel and Law, between aliveness and deadness. In contemporary terms, it is the tension between the organismic strivings for integration, development, and growth, on the one hand, and societal pressures for standardized behavior—for "normality"—on the other, even when this means the violation of inner integrity and wholeness. Though this tension is reflected in the writings and preachments of Paul, he never resolved the tension adequately enough to take a definitive stand on either side. Consequently, our legacy from Paul is at best a confusing array of ambiguities in which, unfortunately, the negative overtones and undertones predominate. The fact that Paul wrote in expectancy of the immediate second coming of Christ merely puts his thinking in proper perspective and does not add to its validity. In fact, it is precisely the context of Paul's thinking, which was grossly misled and misleading, that should prevent us from taking very seriously much, though certainly not all, of what he said about the human condition. In the same sense, to understand that Freud came out of nineteenth-century, mechanistic, physical-chemical, reductionistic science

---

[4] See the very useful chapter "Gestalt Therapy: A Behavioristic Phenomenology," by Elaine Kepner and Lois Brien in Fagan and Shepherd, *Gestalt Therapy Now*, pp. 39-46.

helps us to understand the limitations of Freud's philosophy of man for the twentieth century.

Body, Reality, and Selfhood

The creation myth upon which we focused in Chapter 1 is important, then, because it helps us to recover our authentic heritage in regard to understanding human nature. This heritage reflects the unity, completeness, and totality of human nature and existence without degrading or apologizing for any aspect of it; indeed, without even speaking of any aspect as if it were separated from the whole. Erich Fromm has taught us that one of the needs arising from the conditions of man's existence is the need for *rootedness*. Man needs to feel firmly related to and grounded in his environment; he wants to be an integral part of his world, to feel that he belongs. The man who is fragmented into mind versus body, or who becomes disembodied in acquiescence to the devaluation of materiality and substantiality in our culture, not only feels separated from himself, but also feels estranged from the world. As a totality, man is a glorious representation of creation (of an organism-environment unity) and also of creativity, because he feels himself to be an active agent of his existence, capable of deciding upon the shape and form of his life and of his world. As a collection of various fragments, man feels like a rootless drifter, who does not belong in his world because he does not belong, or feel at home, in his body. In fragmentation, man is out of touch with the body, the medium which mediates actuality, and the assumptive world assumes priority. In other words, instead of living wholesomely in a self and in a world based upon the experience of instinctual and biological urges, sensations, perceptions, and needs, the individual who is fragmented becomes imprisoned in a self and a world based on

49

assumptions, expectations, and images that are faded from reality. He is a thing adrift in a self he does not know and in a world he has not made.

Poor contact with reality is a logical consequence of a dualism which denigrates the physical, material realm of existence. Insofar as the body is the only means whereby reality is experienced, it is valid to say that man *is* his body. However, since out of an anti-sex attitude we tend to identify the body as a mere sexual machine, denial of the body has become a kind of religious regimen in this culture. Even the desire to touch and to be touched is frowned upon, for fear that touching will have only sexual meanings. In a truly religious act, sacrifice or denial of the body implies a prior full acceptance, upon which is based a free decision or choice to use the body, or life-energy, in the service of some purpose to which one commits himself. Gestalt therapy points out that a gift derives from surplus, and is thus given for its own sake because the giver chooses, from his bounty, to bestow a good upon another, whereas a *bribe* is given with the intention of securing approval, praise, obligation, or love. The giver of a bribe will let it be known, in some way, that he could not afford the gift, or that it is one of his favorite articles which he gives up with great reluctance, or that the article is given merely as part of an exchange and not for its own sake. Much of our denial of the body represents veiled attempts to bribe our parents, or society, or God into giving us something in return for our "goodness." The point is, as Laura Perls puts it, that "only he who *has* and *is* can *give*," [5] and anyone who claims to be making a sacrifice of a body from which he is alienated, or of an artifact that is not an "extension" of the self, is simply deceiving himself, as well as anyone who thinks that he can receive a genuine gift from such a person.

[5] Fagan and Shepherd, p. 126.

Society, like the individual, is concerned with smooth, holistic functioning, and prescribes ways of controlling bodily sensations in order to prevent inappropriate behavior. Perhaps, more accurately, society is merely interested in controlling behavior. However, society tends to be so diffuse and ambiguous in its prescriptions and proscriptions that individuals become afraid of their sensations, urges, perceptions, and needs. Society often oversteps its bounds and presumes to pass laws governing any and all expressions of bodily needs. For example, there are still statutes in practically every state of our country which make sexual intercourse between husband and wife illegal in certain rooms of the house. Some laws stipulate that husband and wife may not participate in sexual intercourse on the living room couch. While anachronistic and unenforced, these laws are still on the books, and equally ludicrous laws are still being passed. The result is that these prescriptions and proscriptions tend to become generalized and relations involving the body become ungratifying, mechanical relations in which persons are detached from themselves, and in which they treat both themselves and others as objects, rather than as persons. For various reasons, and in many ways, we have succeeded in making the body—this natural, self-regulating unity and magnificent work of art—into a source of needless frustration and agony. The medium of experience and ecstasy has become the source of human degradation and shame, for human beings, when split, become capable of monstrous things. The solution is not, as some would suppose, the tyranny of the body; the solution is reintegration of mind and body (or soul and body), the only means of restoring the inner unity, integrity, and wholeness (characterized by harmony of thought, feeling, and act) which defines man as a *human* being.

Fritz Perls points out that our mentality is determined

more by instincts than by reason.[6] It is important to note here that the word "instincts" is used broadly to mean tendency, impulse, intuition, need, and so on, rather than in the narrower sense in which Freud, for example, tended to use it to mean impulsion toward a single stimulus through a natural, unacquired mode of response. However, while the human being is capable of deciding how to respond to and how to fulfill his needs, there is nevertheless an automatic quality about certain sensations and urges, such as hunger, thirst, sexual tension, which makes it appropriate to speak of them as instinctual. More explicitly, the child does not *decide* that he derives pleasure from his genitals; he *discovers* this fact and learns, through interaction with others, what means of expression will lead to ultimate fulfillment of his instinctual sexual needs and what will lead to rejection, punishment, alienation, and displeasure. In other words, man's capacity to symbolize frees him from "blind instinct" and allows him not only to choose the means whereby he will fulfill a need or desire, but also to choose to delay gratification until he acquires the things he prefers in order to fulfill the need. For example, if the individual experiences thirst, he may conjure up the image of a soda pop, a beer, a glass of wine, a cocktail, or a glass of water. He may choose, therefore, to seek one of these to fulfill his particular thirst, and if he chooses a beer he may pass up several water fountains until he reaches a bar or his refrigerator at home and can have the beer. Indeed, the person may not even be aware of the water fountains because they do not enter his "field." He may, however, be aware of every billboard that advertises beer because the desire for the beer is sharp figure against dull background. The point is that these symbolic, mental processes derive from the body's instinctual need for fluid to replenish

[6] *Ego, Hunger, and Aggression* (Vintage Book; New York: Random House, 1969), p. 81.

the cells. When the need is met, the unfinished situation (thirst) is finished; another need, interest, or desire will emerge. Such knowledge has turned mothers away from scheduled feedings of infants, patterns which were based on the "rational" way in which adults had learned to schedule their lives, including their most emotional experiences. Pediatricians now advise mothers to feed babies when they are hungry, no matter how frequent or infrequent this may be, for we now know that in such matters we can trust the body to regulate itself.

If we can learn to trust intuition, the intelligence or wisdom of the body, a fascinating thing happens to our imagination (imagery) and symbolization (symbols). We discover the poet in ourselves; namely, the innate ability in each of us to form images which express our experience and which clarify our needs and aid us in meeting them. By establishing the conditions in which people who "cannot draw, cannot paint, cannot sculpture," and so on, make their private symbols and images live, art therapists have demonstrated beyond question that there is an innate creativity in each of us. Movement therapists have made graceful acrobats and interpretive dancers out of people who are awkward, clumsy, self-conscious, and modest by helping them to rediscover and re-own their bodies. And, of course, in dreams we are capable of being and doing all kinds of exciting—and sometimes frightening —things, and our images are numberless. In our dreams we are all poets, dancers, actors, inventors, philosophers, statesmen, troubadours, cowards, heroes, tramps, and so forth, *ad infinitum*. Yet, since we have denied our bodies, the medium of instincts and emotions, our innate intelligence has become intellectualism, which Perls characterizes as "an attitude designed to avoid being deeply moved." [7] Thus, the ever-present

---

[7] *Ibid.*, p. 85.

needs of the body are avoided only at the expense of the holistic function.

In his *Principles of Psychology*, William James pointed out the usefulness of habit in the psychic economy of human existence.[8] We can and do learn to do some things "automatically" and therefore to take them for granted. Perls uses the example of learning to drive an automobile in order to explain this phenomenon in Gestalt terms. In learning to drive, one practices the shifting of gears, steering, braking until they become automatic and can be done without thinking, that is, unawares. However, at the slightest sign that one's driving technique is inadequate, or that the car is operating improperly, or that one is caught in hazardous driving conditions, the driving situation emerges as a "figure" to which attention must be directed. Attention is directed only to that which matters, and whatever matters will emerge from the background, or will become emergency, and thereby demand attention. The analogy holds regarding the body and psychic life. The person who lives in, and therefore feels at home in, his body will not be characterized by hypochrondriacal preoccupation with his body. Rather he will be capable of listening to the messages of the body when the body signals his attention through pain, tension, excitement, or fatigue.

Through the avoidance of the body, we initiate and sustain a civil war in our self which leads to phoniness and deadness. It is not inaccurate to say that the plight of contemporary Western man is summed up in his continual striving for aliveness and meaning in the face of pressures toward the mummification of human personality. There is a restlessness in our self that continually calls our attention to those aspects of our existence which are essential to integrity and authen-

[8] (New York: Henry Holt, 1892; Harper & Row, 1961), pp. 5-17. Gordon Allport edited and wrote the introduction for the reprint edition.

ticity. There is a continual striving in human nature for vitality, creativity, integration, and growth. The source of this striving and restlessness in human nature is the soul of man, which includes his "animal nature"; it is the soul which informs existence with meaning.

The life task of the individual is to learn how to maintain integrity and to become authentic within society without being alienated from it. It is improbable that society will ever be altered *en masse*, either through religious, political, or psychological efforts. However, it is probable that if enough individuals learn to integrate the polarities of existence—such as love and hate; caution and risk; certainty and ambiguity; separateness and relatedness; agency and communion—they will be able to utilize energy, hitherto applied to the maintenance of a good, fixed character, in the development of a society which will support, rather than destroy, uniqueness and individuality. In other words, if persons come to experience themselves as free, active agents of their existence, rather than as imprisoned, passive things whose existence is shaped by others, we can hope for the development of a wholesome society. If not, the demonic nature of human existence will simply intensify.

Human, Animal, Demon

The notion persists, in spite of overwhelming evidence to the contrary, that being human is the opposite of being animal. In an attempt to understand what it means to be human, we make the mistake of assuming that man's animal nature is the source of his inhumanity, a euphemism for brutality, cruelty, and oppression. As animal, man is, in a real sense, merely an inspirited creature, not unlike other creatures. He is one among the swarm of living souls that fill the earth. In short, he is a living, moving, vibrant creature, continually bombarded by needs, urges, and instincts, on the basis of which he shapes his existence. However, as human, man is characterized by a twofold self-awareness which makes him more than animal. He is aware of himself as a unique individual, and he is aware of his potential death. His awareness of himself as a unique individual includes the capacity to experience himself as an active agent who, through the freedom to choose, decide, and respond, is able to create, participate in, and assume responsibility for his destiny. As human, man is capable of remembering the past, anticipating the future, and utilizing these memories and anticipations in the continual re-creation of himself in the ongoing, present process of life.

Problems develop in human existence when one begins to take himself too seriously. More accurately, when one begins to overinvest himself in the images and roles which either aid in the doing of certain tasks or derive from others' expectations and demands, he begins to lose life's essentially playful attitude upon which the open, imaginative creative life is based. He begins to refuse to play with life's possibilities and to take reasonable risks, and he sinks into a style of conformity and hence of mediocrity. At this point, the individual is no longer the agent of his life; he is a passive "thing," possessed by the expectations and demands of the authorities and admired persons whom he has introjected. The person is possessed, as it were, by demons, and the real opposite of the human is the demonic. The demoniac, no longer a person, is a thing, a passive entity that feels no responsibility for its activity, whether positive or negative; constructive or destructive; good or evil. Since he feels no sense of self-containment, and has no sense of boundaries which define him and delineate him from others (since, in other words, he does not know who or what he is), the demoniac is incapable of relating to others or to the environment in any authentic way. The demoniac has given up—in some cases, has never possessed—the power to decide and to act freely on his own terms and, therefore, to be responsible (response-able) for the consequences of his decisions and actions. Feeling separated from his *real* self, the demoniac feels that whatever he does, thinks, or feels is not the will of his real self, but of something or someone that impels him to think his thoughts, feel his emotions, and do his acts. Hence, the demoniac tends to speak in terms of "it" rather than "I" and to feel guilty or uneasy about saying *I*. To speak in the first person is to accept responsibility for one's experience and for what one does or fails to do about that experience. When one says *I*, he chooses an identity; he accepts a name and a face, and the emptiness of his existence begins to be filled with the ability to respond to life. The man whom nobody knew must now be accountable for what he is and for what he does; no longer can others be blamed or praised for his existence. Whenever the demoniac is caught in the act of navel-gazing, it is for the purpose, not of contemplating the meaning of existence, but of marveling at the invisible umbilicus which has never been detached.

The human being is capable of responding uniquely to each emerging need or stimulus, rather than reacting on the basis of a "natural, unmediated response" in a predictable, stereotyped fashion. The human being can decide *how* he will deal with his experience. Hence, the purpose of religious experience, psychotherapy, and education is, instead of adjustment, the exorcism of demons, in submission to which the individual alienates his capacity for active agency. Religious experience, psychotherapy, and education must deal. each in its own way, with the soul and must restore to the individual the ability to move with changing situations while maintaining a measure of stability. They must help the individual to be responsible for his own choices and decisions and to base them upon his actual experience, rather than upon the presumptive and assumptive expectations of others.

A good example of the exorcism of demons is found in the biblical narrative regarding the Gerasene demoniac who was restored to wholeness by Jesus (Mark 5:1-20). The first action of this narrative of exorcism is Jesus' attempt to aid the individual in rediscovering a sense of personal identity. Jesus asks, "What is your name?" The demoniac replies, "My name is Legion; for we are many." He does not know who he is, and in his distorted existence he has come to feel comfortable with his demons: "And he begged him eagerly not to send them out of the country." Yet, when the demoniac meets Jesus with the words, "I adjure you by God, do not torment me," I sense the meaning of the following question, "Are you also (that is, in addition to all the others) going to torment me?" Jesus' question "What is your name?" is, then, a response to this hidden question, for as Ross Snyder puts it:

> I have a name.
>
> My parents gave me the beginning of a name.
> They told the world, "Here is a person. He has a place among human beings." . . .
>
> People call me by name.
>
>> By this they say, "I want you to be present." Sometimes it wonderfully means "Hello there, freedom."
>>
>> When a person calls to me by name, he is admitting me into the circle of people he recognizes as fellow-human. Into his cluster of people who believe in each other.
>
> My name is shorthand for the fact that I mean something. . . .
>
> When people call me by name, I know that I am something distinctive. Irreplaceable. Original poetry of the present. This *particular*

vitality. A truth or falsehood that appears
to them. A destiny.

O that I never become a number.

Or be anonymous in situations where I
should be a name, and not be a blur.°

To be possessed by demons is to have lost a clear sense of who
one is, to be unable to say, "I am I." Therefore, demons cannot be exorcised unless the exorcist has as his first premise
that he must accept the other person as he is, aid him in the
recovery of his true self, and eschew attempts and temptations to make him over in his own image. There is a very
thin line that separates the process of removing introjects
from that of merely becoming another introject. The alleged
exorcist—be he priest, therapist, or educator, and no matter
how healthy, wholesome, and creative—who loses sight of
this line merely becomes another demon, squashing down
even more the warped existence of the imprisoned, tormented
self.

In the second place, the narrative makes it clear that the
demons, though pleading to be driven into the swine, cannot
live in any creature without precipitating self-destruction. In
the human sphere, demonic possession not only destroys or
de-structures the self, but also instates self-destruction as a
way of life. The exorcism of demons is, therefore, a process
of aiding the person in the utilization of energy for actualizing
human potentialities in lieu of destroying himself. Only thus
can human dignity be recovered, and this dignity includes
a sense of responsibility in which one takes and develops in
himself what he is and what he can be. Notice that in the
biblical story this process is frightening to the townsmen. I
suggest that they were frightened not only because of the

° "Calling a Person by Name," *Inscape* (Nashville: Abingdon Press,
1968), pp. 53-55.

mystery of the occurrence, and of the power and authority of Jesus' personal presence—that is, his presence as a person to another (potential) person—but also because of the transformation of the demoniac into a strong, integrated, developing person, who was no longer weak, predictable, and fragmented and who stood as a commentary on their own fragmentation. The townsmen can no longer project their fears, uncertainties, and self-alienation onto the demoniac with impunity, for with his new strength the demoniac will undoubtedly challenge them to come to terms with themselves. It is awesome when those about us cease to be predictable and therefore controllable, for then we find that we must respond afresh to each person and to each event, and in the process *we* must change. The exorcist, then, must be something of an iconoclast who does not fear change and challenge; yet, he must be an unselfconscious iconoclast, lest the iconoclastic image become the important thing to him.

Finally, the process of exorcising demons is complete only when true community (in contrast to the *false* community of demonic possession) is restored through genuine encounter. Since sin is a state—namely, a state of alienation from oneself and therefore from others—before it is an act, repentance is a return to one's true self. When one feels secure in his separateness as a unique individual, he is capable of encounter with those who matter. In psychological language: having made contact with one's authentic self in the safe, experimental situation of the therapeutic contract, the individual must test the measure and validity of his growth and strength in the daily issues of life and death with significant others. For this reason, when the former demoniac asks permission to accompany Jesus, he is told to go home and to encounter his friends. I suspect that Jesus was at least slightly sarcastic when he said: "Go home to your friends, and tell them how much the Lord has done for you, and how he [unlike them] has had mercy on you." Ross Snyder says, in a discussion of "The Thisness of a Person":

> Who is the person sitting next to you?
>
>> You might say a name. Describe how tall he is, and the color of eyes and hair.
>>
>> But none of these things are what the person is. A person is invisible activities. . . .
>>
>> Deep within this person is a great toughness for his own integrity—a tenacity in the face of adversity. Human nature is the most indestructible thing that we know . . . it goes on surviving in the midst of unbelievable difficulties and persecutions. A person is an overpowering will to be, to attain completion, to arrive at destinations. . . .
>
> He is a need to reveal himself . . . to be known even as he knows himself . . . at a level deeper than words.
>
> The person nearest you is a unique world of experience. . . . He is the only person in the whole world in direct touch with how he feels, sees, experiences. . . .
>
>> He can live not only for himself, but also for you. He can confront, understand you— if that is what you want. In turn, he is to be understood. And unless he is understood by other people, he is thwarted from being a person. . . .

He can never be fully understood. He is more than any description or explanation—or your perception of him. He can never be fully controlled—nor should be. You cannot violate him with impunity. He is one of the great mysteries you will meet in your life.[10]

True encounter then is a meeting of opposites or separates;

[10] *Inscape*, pp. 37-43.

true relatedness or contact presumes an appreciation of differences. The mature person knows that differences do not mean that relatedness is impossible; instead, differences mean that the relatedness which is fertilized will be mutually enriching for the participants. This is why the testing ground of the demoniac's transformation must be his relationships with significant others who, though previously introjects, must now be challenged in the I-Thou encounter.

On the one hand, I am tempted to apologize for this slightly homiletical approach. On the other hand, I am pleased to have discovered this biblical narrative which delineates some important features of the objectives and the conditions of change of Gestalt therapy, which I hope will become clear in the next chapter.

In passing, I want to point out that institutions, like individuals, can and do become demonic in the following ways: First, when the human use of institutions is replaced by the institutional use of humans. For example, in the name of tradition, policy, legal stipulations, and so on, we often sacrifice our last iota of integrity and personhood and become puppets who look, think, and act like every other worker, when with a few reasonable risks we could aid in the revival of dead institutions, which have died in their uselessness and mummification. Second, we often feel powerless to effect necessary change in institutions, even when such change is demanded by human need and changing circumstances; and, lest we be spurned by the other mummies, we fail to risk conflict, mistakes, and suffering in order to satisfy even our vision of change. Unfortunately, when cowardice persists long enough, we even lose our visionary capacities; we become merely passive. Third, we allow technology to supplant personhood, and in this context authority is repressively misused to thwart the development of human potential and to protect the "machine" or system.

In the individual sphere, the life task is to learn how to actualize the self and thereby to contribute to the humanness of society; to become a separate person, who can relate to, and not be possessed by, others; to be capable of authentic encounter with others without desiring to possess them; to be able to stand alone without taking this to mean loneliness. No man can possess another, in any sense, without enslaving himself, for in the act of possession one imprisons himself in an unholy alliance which cannot be dissolved until the possessed claims his freedom. When, through tyranny of any form, psychological or ideological, one succeeds in obliterating human individuality, both victor and victim are dehumanized. In the institutional sphere the task is to restore institutions to their rightful status as human agencies, shaped, and formed by, and serving human agents. The task of the healer, be he priest, therapist, or teacher, is the exorcism of individual and corporate demons in the service of humanness.

Humanity or humanness does not obliterate or degrade man's animal nature. Humanity merely gives the animal nature of a man a peculiar stamp, so that the liveliness, vitality, excitability, and instinctual and biological urges which define animality may be used in humans to different ends than those to which they are put by other creatures. With men, for example, there is no mating season in which male and female are compelled to couple willy-nilly. Rather, man's capacity for sexual response is ever present, and man's capacity to symbolize the consequences or results of his actions makes it possible for him to make a free choice and decision about how to respond to his needs and desires. The foundation of selfhood is precisely the awareness of instinctual and biological urges, upon which are based one's sense of separateness and self-propulsion, if you will. When the infant becomes aware of these urges and begins to learn that they will not always be satisfied by others (initially the parents), that he must learn to gratify them for himself, and that he will have to delay gratifying them at times for various reasons, he is learning what it means to be a separate, unique individual. It is, in other words, a proper balance of frustration and support from the parent that allows the child to move from the confluence and symbiosis characteristic of the early parent-child microcosm to the contact and relatedness demanded in the macrocosm of maturing persons.

Only when man's animality (not animalism) is understood and accepted as a part of the totality of human nature can the striving for authentic humanity be fulfilled. Only then will the total organism be accepted as the medium through which man experiences and creates his reality. "At-one-ment" with oneself and with one's world is impossible if one avoids his animal nature, his body. In this conception, estrangement is the fragmentation of existence through the spurious dichotomies of mind and body, spirit and body, and soul and body, which can be separated only for the purposes of discussion. *Sin*, then, refers, first and foremost, to a condition or state of existence characterized by a feeling of rootlessness and subsequent desperation from which proceed poor choices and decisions, misguided feelings, and acts which are destructive to oneself and to others. The emphasis here is on what one is, rather than on what one does—especially if the doing is judged in reference to codes and dogmas which presume to specify behavior for every human situation. More accurately, the emphasis here is on *how* one expresses who and what he *is*, in and through what he *does*.

The "Fall": Fragmentation and Alienation

The mythical "fall" of man, then, helps to clarify what it means to be human. In the creation myth, the man and the woman are created as total organisms, as psychophysical unities. Their fragmentation is depicted as deriving from their desire to acquire knowledge by ingesting the forbidden fruit. When his act is discovered, the human being expresses his demonic potential by projecting the responsibility for his act upon the serpent. Among the man, the woman, and the serpent, a cult of blame is instituted. At this point, the implication of the narrative is that man avoided his medium of experience, namely, his organism or self, and sought the easy acquisition of awareness of all experience through the utopian, magical means of merely ingesting fruit (just as some persons ingest drugs with an expectation of magical growth). The limits had been made clear to man, though the possibilities for his violation of the limits were not removed. Perhaps, more accurately, the narrative suggests that prior to eating the fruit man was deliriously unaware of himself as a unique creature and only afterwards became aware of his peculiar potentialities. Perhaps it is at this point that man becomes truly human, for in the act of violating the limits man discovers what it means to move from the safety, security, and confluence of "paradise" to the pain, frustration, conflict, and anguish of separate, human existence. At the moment that man discovers that he can observe and accuse another as a separate being, he becomes aware that he also can be observed, and is accountable, both for what he is and for what he does. As long as he tries to avoid responsibility for his activity, man feels ashamed, and, when he acknowledges his act, he becomes aware of his genitalia, which are the supreme symbols of his agential capacity to create new life and to participate in the ongoing creation of the world and also the symbols of his communal need for mutual nurture, stimulation, and interdependency. As in the narrative, also in actual life the human being moves from symbiotic dependence, through separation and independence, to the communion of interdependence, in which dependence and independence are wholesomely united.

65

Man's fall can be understood, then, as his separation from the center of his existence in an attempt to achieve the knowledge that can only come from his acceptance of "at-home-ness" within himself. Life is, consequently, a continual pilgrimage in search of a lost unity. We long to return to "paradise lost," and we forget that only when paradise was lost did man become aware of himself as a separate being with unique, peculiar potentialities. Even at the origin of human experience, it was conflict, anguish, and suffering that brought new awareness. Hence, whatever measure of paradise is regained—and this is at best a momentary phenomenon in human experience—is contingent upon our residing in our bodies, for, when the holistic function of life is distorted, we inevitably fall prey to either purely psychologistic or purely naturalistic approaches which require avoidance of essential aspects of human nature, and which are inadequate for orienting us to life as wholeness and integrity.

In summary, the denial of the body condemns us to attempting to experience reality through the mind, or through some other truncated approach to existence. The point is that while the logic of the mind is useful in scientific and technological activity, this logic can never be adequate for understanding human existence in its wholeness, for in this understanding only the logic of the soul (psycho-logic) applies. Or in the words of Hillman, the Jungian analyst:

> An analyst faces problems, and these problems are not merely classifiable behavioural acts, nor medical categories of disease. *They are above all experiences and sufferings, problems with an 'inside'.* The first thing that the patient wants from an analyst is to make him aware of his suffering and to draw the analyst into his world of experience. Experience and suffering are terms long associated with soul.[11]

When we attempt to frame human existence with the logical

[11] *Suicide and the Soul*, pp. 43-44.

categories of the mind, the results are intellectualizations which more often obscure rather than express or clarify reality; rigid value-systems which betray insecurities in the face of the ambiguities of existence; hysterical quests for excitement and stimulation which, when found, never fully satisfy, and so on. When man is ungrounded in himself, his existence is unstable, his experience vague, and his reality faded, and he becomes capable of monstrous things in order to feel secure, to have some experience, and to maintain an assumptive reality. (When we talk about human groundedness, it is particularly interesting to note, in the light of Chapter 1, that the word "human" is related to both *homo,* man, and *humus,* soil.)

In contemporary Western culture our loss of contact is experienced as a sense of emptiness. We use and maintain our bodies, and yet consider the important things to be the vaguely defined realms of the mind, the spirit, and the soul. Psychologists can accurately speak of us then as disembodied spirits in forsaken bodies. It is difficult for us to understand the necessary unity of thought, emotion, and act, as the basis of effective and gratifying living. Therefore, since our activity is based largely upon abstractions and removed from organismic experience, we are unable to feel deeply, think soundly, or act effectively. We are extremely uncomfortable with joy, anger, grief, or orgasm, those unified experiences of emotion, thinking, and action which signal completion, fulfillment, and restoration. Yet, the absence of these genuine explosions makes all the more ominous the probability of such artificial explosions as homicide, suicide, wars, and nuclear experiments which pollute the environment.

We are presently immobilized by a self-imposed and self-sustained fragmentation and deadness. We have split ourselves into a blessed half (soul) and a damned half (body), and have projected the responsibility for healing the split upon our parents, or society, or God. And when the split is not healed externally, we conclude that it is inevitable, sink into an attitude of quietism, and wait for the apocalypse, when "paradise lost" allegedly will be regained, once for all, without any effort on our parts—unless, of course, we have been "alive" during our existence, in which case we will have to endure purgatory for a while to be cleansed of our "worldliness," or we will have to endure eternal torment forever—depending upon your theology. I want to suggest that the split will be healed only when we freely decide to endure the pain and suffering in the here and now which are inevitable in the process of change and growth. Moreover, even if we succeed in laying aside the burden of Hellenistic dualism, we will discover that a state of redemption, finalized and complete, exists nowhere and never. Life is rather a continuing series of unfinished situations; and in the finishing of these situations, the completing of incomplete gestalts, we experience the excitement of living and discover hitherto unrealized potential. Life is a perpetual process of change and growth, death and rebirth, which is terminated only by actual death, at least so far as we know, and in which, fortunately, we occasionally experience moments of rest and restoration on utopian or blissful plateaus (moments without which existence undoubtedly would be intolerable).

Organismic Experience and the Symbolization Process

When body awareness recedes, reality is faded and the emerging images have no meaningful, experiential referents, for, as Alexander Lowen says;

> Normally, the image is a reflection of reality, a mental construction which enables the person to orient his movement for more effective action. In other words, the image mirrors the body. When, however, the body is inactive, the image becomes a sub-

stitute for the body, and its dimensions expand as body awareness recedes.[12]

As body awareness recedes, leaving the body feeling empty,
images or symbols proliferate to fill the void. Yet the images,
having no connection to reality with which the body is in
contact, become mere intellectualizations, rather than intelli-
gent and intelligible representations of reality. Such images
do not aid in effecting closure, and existence based on such
images invariably becomes a stockpile of unfinished situations.
These images are not assimilated and made part of the self;
they are simply held on to, and they become more and more
sacrosanct in and of themselves. Ultimately, elaborate theories
and dogmas are created to explain images which originated
out of a faded or blurred reality.

Gestalt therapy points out that the unfulfilling image
is based on part projection, whereas creativity is total projection, total participation in and identification with one's
images. In total projection, one creates his own reality, based
on his actual organismic experience, rather than allowing a
faded reality to press icons upon him which have no meaning.

I am ready now to consider Gestalt therapy in terms of its
relationship to what I have said thus far. Gestalt therapy is
a valuable contribution to our efforts to understand what it
means to be human, or rather what we mean as humans. The
point I have tried to make so far is that the Gestalt or holistic
approach to life is our heritage from ancient Israel through
the naturalistic and holistic emphasis of its life and culture.
I have tried to understand the soul of Judaism as it applies
to the individual human existence and thus to collective
human experience. Martin Buber asserts that the soul of
Judaism is pre-Sinaitic and patriarchal (that is, it antedates
the Law and systematizing of Moses), and that its funda-

[12] *The Betrayal of the Body* (London: Collier-Macmillan, 1969), pp.
6-7.

mental attitude of unification, integrity, and wholeness cannot be understood through the Law received or propounded by Moses on Sinai.[18] The task of Gestalt therapy is to aid the individual to rediscover the fundamental attitude of unification, wholeness, and integrity in his self and in his relatedness to other persons and his world.

One final word before coming to Gestalt therapy. I recognize the danger of romanticism in what I have set forth about ancient Israel's understanding of man and in what I am now proceeding to say about Gestalt therapy. Gestalt therapy has already been romanticized by some persons as the way of life for modern man, though more responsible persons, including the primary developer, Fritz Perls, recognize that Gestalt therapy is, at best, an approach rather than a finished product. In the next chapter, I am attempting to tie together what I understand to be important historical claims regarding the nature of man with the contemporary expressions of these claims, in a unique and exciting way, in Gestalt therapy. If, in the process, I can make some contribution to our efforts to understand, and to improve, the development of human nature, I shall be pleased.

[18] *Israel and the World* (New York: Schocken Books, 1963), pp. 7-8.

... life force first mobilizes the center. And the center of the personality is what used to be called the soul: the emotions, the feelings, the spirit.

To suffer one's death and to be reborn is not easy.—Fritz Perls, *Gestalt Therapy Verbatim*

III

GESTALT THERAPY: CHANGE AND GROWTH

Just as Genesis 2 is clear that man is a totality whose nature is distorted by dualisms, Gestalt therapy is clear that man is a total organism, functioning as a whole rather than as a thing split into fragments such as mind and body. In its emphasis on the unity of emotion and act, on aliveness and deadness as measures of one's participation in his existence, on the critical nature of the here-and-now, I-and-thou encounter, and on the significance of every mode through which one expresses his being-in-the-world (even such *obvious* modes as facial expressions and gestures), Gestalt therapy is a statement in contemporary language of the naturalism and holism which characterized the life and culture of ancient Israel. Therapeutically, however, the Gestalt approach is as unique and peculiar as the therapist is creative, for each individual who uses this approach must choose and develop a style that best fits him and that expresses who he is and who he is becoming. In this discussion of the theory and method of Gestalt therapy, I want to place particular emphasis on the significance of frustration, conflict, pain, and suffering in the process of human growth and development.

Organismic Self-Regulation

Gestalt therapy formulates a concept of the natural rhythm of organismic equilibrium-disequilibrium and asserts that the disequilibrium becomes normative only when essential aspects of the self are alienated, denied, and controlled in deference to ideals, mores, customs, and demands which either are figments of our fantasy, or are actually imposed by society. The natural rhythm is what Gestalt therapy calls *organismic self-regulation*. Simkin points out that if we can survive the continual attempts of others to civilize or enslave us into rigid and anti-self patterns of existence, we pick and choose from the environment what we need to support ourselves or to fulfill ourselves.[1] If we mobilize sufficient aggression—the means whereby contact is achieved—to choose, chew up, swallow, and assimilate what we find palatable, rather than what significant or dominant others tell us we *ought* to choose, then the self is gratified, or restored to equilibrium, and the foreground is clear for the emergence into awareness of another figure from the organismic background. In other words, when closure is effected in one situation, the person can be open to emerging situations, to what is coming into being. Whereas, when closure is not effected, when there is unfinished business, the person is fixated on what-has-been, and blocks what-is-coming-into-being. In marriage, for example, when resentments are not expressed, each spouse becomes diligent in atempting to convict the other of wrongdoing and to make him feel guilty, and thus the unexpressed resentments block the intimacy which could emerge if they were expressed

[1] James S. Simkin, "Introduction to Gestalt Therapy" (Cleveland: Cleveland Gestalt Institute), p. 2.

and worked through so that closure could be effected. When we become fixated on ideals, we tyrannize ourselves by standards and guidelines which not only are remote from our actual experience, but also require the avoidance of our experience. One of my friends, who is married and the mother of two children, reports that when she jokingly referred in a letter to her mother to the mate-swapping that recently has become rather faddish, she received in reply a written lecture from her mother, the gist of which was, "You should not allow yourself even to think about such a thing!" The mother's misleading and misled assumption is that if one is unaware of what he thinks, feels, and desires, he is better able to control his behavior. The fact is that when one keeps his actual experience out of awareness he makes himself a passive slave of this experience, in some basic way.

The irony of external and internal attempts to civilize us at all costs is in the demand that we subdue, deny, or control instinctual tendencies, lest through our full participation and unabated enthusiasm they become uncontrollable and overwhelming. This illusion is, of course, a product of the mind-body dualism which alleges that the mind, representing man's "higher" nature, must control the body, representing man's link to other creatures and hence his "lower" nature. The demand for control, ostensibly intended to aid in the maintenance of a measure of stability as the individual flows with his experience, ultimately aids in the maintenance of the status quo, based on the fear that the self, if allowed free rein, will run wild in orgiastic preoccupation with its selfish concerns and that society will be damaged, if not destroyed. (We tend to discuss control in explicitly sexual terms.) Abraham Maslow points out that "dichotomizing pathologizes (and pathology dichotomizes). Isolating two interrelated parts of a whole from each other, parts that need each other, parts

73

that are truly 'parts' and not wholes, distorts them both, sickens and contaminates them." [2]

Gestalt therapy posits that only the expression of a need and not the need itself can be suppressed and that the unexpressed need results in unfinished situations in the organism-environment field. In numerous experiments, Gestalt psychologists have demonstrated that the unfinished task is remembered better than the finished task and that unfinished tasks seem to create a restlessness in the person until he can complete the tasks. It follows, then, that the commonsense approach of self-denial and self-control leads to numerous preoccupations through the stockpiling of unfinished situations in the personality. Contrary to the commonsense understanding, preoccupations result from the innate striving of human nature for completion, for development, for growth, rather than from an inherently evil, animalistic nature of man which makes him uncontrollable.

The demand of *conscientious avoidance* is a double-bind of the worst sort, requiring that one be diligently aware of precisely what he is to avoid. Stated differently, one is to be preoccupied with, or fixated upon, what he is not supposed to allow into awareness or to express. This kind of double-bind is enough to drive people crazy, and it often does just that. However, in its conception of *organismic self-regulation*, Gestalt therapy frees individuals from this double-bind. When a need is expressed (and expression may occur on a continuum from merely admitting into full awareness one's needs, interests, or desires to total activity in a unity of thought, feeling, and act), equilibrium is restored and the sensory-motor apparatus of the self is freely available for participation in the emerging reality.

[2] *Religions, Values, and Peak-Experiences* (Columbus: Ohio State University Press, 1964), p. 13.

Ontology and Phenomenology in Gestalt Therapy

Through its rapproachement of theory and therapy, Gestalt therapy is an exciting philosophy of life that can be tested and elaborated continually. In America, there is generally little or no essential connection between the various theories and the methods which undergird psychotherapy. American psychotherapies are usually verbal, the theories being more conceptual than phenomenological. In basically conceptual schemes, it is necessary to attempt to fit the data to the conceptions, for it is difficult to deal with, or even to be fully aware of, data which contradict the system. Conceptual systems generally attempt to achieve complete, finalized closure and become closed systems by explaining new data in terms of the presuppositions and a priori conclusions of the system. Contrariwise, open systems are not primarily interested in vindicating the conceptual framework by fitting all new data to the conceptions; instead, open systems use the conceptual framework as an orienting tool, to be enlarged, corrected, and perhaps totally revised as new data demand. In this way, open systems avoid becoming rigid, orthodox, and sterile.

Gestalt therapy combines ontology and phenomenology. Van Dusen asserts that in every conceptual or classificatory system we tend to preserve the illusion of *a* reality, whereas in a phenomenological approach one encounters strange and radically different *realities* or worlds.[3] Originally formulated by Frederick S. Perls, Gestalt therapy aims to undo self-defeating behavior and to increase human potential by helping the individual to discover his unique interests, needs, and desires. As an existential philosophy, Gestalt therapy starts and ends with the organism. Ontologically, it recognizes

---

[3] Van Dusen, in *American Journal of Psychoanalysis*, XX (1960), 35.

the biological formation of *gestalten* (wholes) as the basis of conceptual activity. For example, the thirsty person conceives of various ways to fulfill his need and forms images which "in-form" or "embody" his activity. Further, Gestalt therapy focuses on organismic experience in order to clarify the semantics of expression. For example, the person who says he is afraid is asked to describe how he experiences his fear bodily. In the process, what the person thought was merely fear might be discovered to be resentment or grief.

> An intellectualizing male graduate student in group therapy announces blandly to no one in particular, "I have difficulty in relating to people." In the ensuing silence, he glances briefly at the attractive nurse who was cotherapist. The therapist immediately asked, "Who *here* do you have trouble relating to?" The student is able to name the nurse, and spends a fruitful five minutes exploring his mixed frustration, attraction, and anger focused on this desirable but inaccessible woman.[4]

The ontological foundation of Gestalt therapy is summed up in the contention that growth is inherent in every organic being. Therefore, the work of facilitating integration involves removing whatever blocks growth, and thereby allowing the individual to fulfill his genuine needs and interests. Phenomenologically, following the motto of Husserl ("to the things themselves"), Gestalt therapy stays close to the sources of experience, which implies attempting to understand oneself and others on the basis of the totality of experience as it is expressed in gestures, voice, posture, motility, breathing, and so on, and not just, or even basically, by focusing on words. By establishing the conditions in which the person may explore all the aspects of his being-in-the-world, Gestalt therapy breaks the verbal chains of psychotherapy and returns to the true source of experience, namely, the psychophysical self in

[4] John Enright, in Fagan and Shepherd, p. 110.

all its modes of being. Hence, though we presently do not know the limits of the further reaches of human awareness and potential, Gestalt therapy, with its ontological foundation and phenomenological approach, and with its existential-humanistic orientation, sets us on the course of clearly understanding and facilitating the development of the essence and potential of human nature.

The Central Conception of Gestalt Therapy

The central conception of Gestalt therapy is that "the organism is striving for the maintenance of a balance which is continuously disturbed by its needs, and regained through their gratification or elimination." [5] The self derives its meaning from within. This is not a simplistic conception of homeostasis, which is generally understood to imply that the desire of the organism is to be totally undisturbed in its existence and that frustration, pain, conflict, and suffering are undesirable. On the contrary, Gestalt therapy's holistic emphasis recognizes the continuous disturbance of organismic balance as inevitable in the process of human growth, and as the key to the continual unfolding of the human personality. Life consists of an infinite number and variety of unfinished situations or incomplete gestalts, and the self is alternately either a gestalt or a fragment-striving-to-become-a-gestalt. To be fully understood, this conception must be viewed in the context of Gestalt therapy's formulation of the ego. Whereas our legacy from orthodox psychoanalysis is an understanding of the ego as a fairly passive substrate of identifications with significant or dominant others, which arbitrates in the con-

[5] Frederick S. Perls, "Gestalt Therapy and Human Potentialities," in *Explorations in Human Potentialities*, ed. Herbert A. Otto (Springfield, Ill.: Charles C. Thomas, 1966). This article was reprinted and distributed by Esalen Institute.

tinual battle between the id and the superego, Gestalt therapy understands the ego as a process or function rather than as a substance. The ego is the process or function of identification (or choosing) and alienation (or rejecting) which occurs at the contact boundary of the organism-environment field. Stated differently, the ego *is* the contact boundary of the organism-environment field which is defined by its identification-alienation functions. The self, then, is not defined by identifications in the Freudian sense, whereby the individual "introjects" significant others into his personality and thereby destroys his individuality. Instead, the self is the total organism as it responds to its environment, or as it chooses and rejects its environment. This conception of the ego and the self is difficult for us to grasp because we have been so overwhelmed by the conception of the *social self*. It is necessary to note that individuality, which we allegedly prize as much as we prize sociality, is based upon the awareness of separating boundaries or differences. In the language of Gestalt therapy, sociality or contact presumes the isolating or separating function of the ego, for the absence of this function results in confluence rather than genuine relatedness.[6] When we understand the formulation of the ego as the choosing-rejecting function of the organism-environment contact boundary, we see that the social-self conception is inadequate for explicating in depth much other than adjustment-oriented therapy. The social-self conception, with its substantive formulation of the ego, is basically conceptual, and attempts to fit the data to the system. On the contrary, the holistic conception, with its functional formulation of the ego, is basically phenomenologi-

[6] The definition or popular understanding of democracy as "the will of the majority," meaning that differences are unwelcome and intolerable, is a good example of confluence. When understood properly, democracy welcomes pluralism and establishes clear limits which guarantee that individual rights will not be infringed and that individuality will be respected.

cal and focuses on how the self chooses or avoids choosing its existence.

Generally, when we speak of the self, we have in mind an image which must be maintained, a delineation which must not be changed, a quantity which must be perpetuated. On the contrary, Gestalt therapy thinks of the self as the total organism, which is striving for completion rather than perpetuation. The emphasis is on self-actualization, which derives from awareness of actual organismic experience, rather than on self-image actualization, which derives from identification with demands and expectations that are perpetrated by others. In the final analysis, Gestalt therapy sees each person as responsible for choosing to be what he is, and if this were not the case, psychotherapy (healing of the soul) would be either a misnomer or a ludicrous, meaningless, and exploitative venture.

Ecological Unity: The Interdependency of the Organism and the Environment

Gestalt therapy's holistic conception obliterates the spurious barrier between the biological (individual) and sociological (social) fields, for the biological field is a part of the sociological field, and vice-versa. The organism (individual) cannot exist without the environment (society), nor the environment without the organism. If the environment neglects or destroys the organism, it loses the organism's participation in the maintenance of ecological balance. If, on the other hand, the organism neglects or destroys the environment, those things which the organism demands for the gratification of its needs and therefore for the restoration of organismic balance will not be available. Hence, ecological unity (whether in the physical or strictly human sphere) is an absolute requirement in the human process of self-completion. It is in recognition of this essential organism-environment unity that Gestalt therapy prefers to speak of the contact-boundary (ego) in the organism-environment field, rather than of "inner" and "outer." I shall have more to say about this later.

In the strictly human sphere, the individual must reckon with the conflict between his needs and the demands of society. Both the individual and society are concerned with smooth holistic functioning. Perls writes: 'Society has to determine which identifications [choices] of the individual are desirable for society's smooth holistic functioning, without damaging the individual's development, its physical and mental health." [7] He adds that this obviously simple task is outside the scope of civilization as we now know it, and that any society that continually violates the conditions of individual development cannot last. In America, current trends, reflecting the notion that individual and social needs are inherently and unalterably opposed, and resulting in standardization of personality, obliteration of individuality, and robotized functioning, are serious omens of a decayed society. When a society forgets that its *raison d'être* is the provision of means whereby individual growth and development are facilitated, it is doomed. The fulfillment of this task, or the maintenance of smooth holistic functioning in the society, is based, as in the individual, on the rhythm of stability and crisis, balance and disturbance, harmony and disharmony. This rhythmic oscillation is the necessary change which ushers in growth, and it is when the attempt is made to maintain the status quo, either individually or corporately, that problems arise. The human self evinces a tropistic striving *away from* that which stagnates and deadens *toward* that which enlivens.

In Gestalt therapy final integration is never reached, but is always in process. The illusion of completeness and inte-

[7] Perls, *Ego, Hunger, and Aggression,* p. 147.

80

gration—at best momentary phenomena in human existence —is a nonsensical notion based on avoidance of the stream of awareness which results in clinging to a rigid self-image or self-concept, a kind of death-in-life. The discovery of new potential and possibility requires the presence of a certain amount of tension, for real gratification and fulfillment is impossible without some tension. Again Perls writes that "the creation of new wholes is not accomplished by fusion but by more or less violent struggles." [8]

The infant provides a useful analogy. At the moment of birth the infant, leaving the nonexistence of the womb, must begin to breathe for himself. Developing in the nurture of parents, he must suck in order to receive sustenance (though this sucking is more or less automatic in early development). Through a progressive series of difficult struggles, frustrations of the symbiotic relationship with the parents, developing capacities which must be utilized, the child learns that he must begin to support himself as his developing resources allow. The process of maturing or self-support continues through pain, frustration, suffering, and crisis, and leads to the discovery that one can do things for himself and, therefore, for others. If loved and nurtured properly, that is, if provided with an adequate balance of support and frustration and not smothered by overprotection or abused by neglect, indifference, and brutality, the child learns that "the harmonious functioning of individual and society depends upon: 'Thou shalt love thy neighbor as thyself.' Not less, but also not more." [9] Thus, the child learns to be a free, self-supporting, self-directing agent who participates in the creation and development of his environment, rather than merely taking from it. He learns not to fear frustration, conflict, and so on, in

[8] *Ibid.*, p. 60.
[9] *Ibid.*, p. 224.

the faith that each frustration-and-integration cycle will un-
earth unused potential and lead to new vistas of life. Since
reality is always tension, risk, and ambiguity, human existence
permits no finality. Human existence is extremely complex,
and ambiguity is inevitable in complex situations. When two
persons are present to each other as I and Thou—which
means they are taking each other's uniqueness and individuality seriously—the complexities and ambiguities of encounter
are merely added to those of individual existence. Finality is
stagnation and death; ambiguity is possibility and life.

Gestalt therapy is not only a diagnosis, but also a remedy
of man's condition, and it shifts from the scientific model to
the humanistic model, from the medical or pathological field
to the educational field. The individual learns *how* he is
blocking his growth and in this awareness learns that he can
change the *how* of his *being*. Hence, therapy becomes an
inadequate term for describing this approach to life. Perls
asserts that sickness is only one form of disordered functioning
and that the medical model is too narrow to be applied to
situations in which fragmentation, alienation, meaninglessness, and deadness derive from existential despair. "The word
'therapy' is actually not quite correct anymore because what
we deal with is not so much illness as disorder. Illness is one
form of inability to cope with the world." [10] Mechanistic,
anti-self, socialization-oriented theories and methods that have
prevailed heretofore have been powerless to deal with the
existential guilt which many persons present and which
grows out of one's despair over failure to actualize his unique
self, instead of a self-image. Mechanistic conceptions, which
are facilely eloquent in explaining various degrees of soci-
opathy, mostly stammer and stutter when faced with the travail of the soul. In the face of existential despair deriving from

[10] Appendix D, p. 186.

the struggle of the unique self for meaning and fulfillment, mechanistic theories, afraid to walk the valley of the shadows wherein the soul may be discovered and reborn, tend to become glibly homiletical or moralistic and to talk about "getting a grip on life" (meaning *consensually validated* reality) and "exercising willpower" (meaning to ignore, rather than to live in and work through the struggle of one's soul). Disordered functioning grows out of the individual's capitulation to the "should" demands of others and leads to the adoption of a fixed character, or a number of stereotyped responses. In this way, the individual becomes a victim of automatic functioning via what Perls calls "the curse of the ideal" [11] and begins to experience himself as a spectator to the *game* of life. He learns to disregard *his* feelings, thoughts, and interests, and thereby loses contact with significant portions and processes of his self, for ideals, when they result from environmental pressures and are not connected with organismic experience, leave one feeling inferior, impotent, and desperate in attempting to actualize them. The fixed character aids in avoiding these feelings of inferiority, impotence, and desperation, only at the expense, however, of petrification of the ego's functions of choosing and rejecting at the organism-environment boundary. Thus, the individual becomes neurotic, or functions in a disorderly fashion, because the functions of the self have been overpowered by the demands of society, whether these demands are real or fancied in the mind of the individual.

In Gestalt therapy, then, neurosis is a disorganization of the proper functioning of the self within its environment, produced by the conflict of the individual's needs and demands with the needs and demands of society. This conflict between society and the individual for the smooth holistic

[11] Frederick S. Perls, *Gestalt Therapy Verbatim* (Lafayette, Calif.: The Real People Press, 1969), p. 19.

functioning of each results in the expenditure of tremendous amounts of energy. Energy that would ordinarily be utilized in meeting and fulfilling the genuine needs of the self is utilized to maintain a phony character and to avoid excitement by imploding and deadening the sensory-motor apparatus of the self. In the societal sphere, energy that ordinarily would be used in establishing the conditions and fulfilling the objectives of change is utilized in maintaining the status quo. The essence of neurotic or disordered functioning, then, is avoidance, mainly the avoidance of contact, with one's self-experience and with one's world, both animate and inanimate.

Gestalt therapy recognizes that only the self can be restored or healed in psychotherapy. Perls writes, "The social norms cannot be altered in psychotherapy, and the instincts cannot be altered at all." [12] Hence, the being-in-the-world of the self, or more specifically *how* the person chooses or avoids his self-experience, is the focus in Gestalt therapy. When the true self is rediscovered in the process of examining the "howness" of one's existence, the individual can then participate authentically in the creation and re-creation of himself and his environment. Only thus can the individual aid society in discovering ways of insuring its holistic functioning without damaging the individual's development and growth via tyranny or stagnation.

Awareness: The Immediate Aim of Gestalt Therapy

The immediate aim of Gestalt therapy is the restoration of awareness, the undoing of avoidance. Here I am not referring

[12] Frederick S. Perls *et al, Gestalt Therapy: Excitement and Growth in the Human Personality* (New York: Dell Publishing Co., 1951), p. 361.

to the extensions of awareness of which man may be capable, though we do know that man is capable of greater awareness than he presently evinces. (Experimentation with psychedelic drugs, for example, has revealed to us some of the possibilities of "expanded" awareness.) The emphasis in Gestalt therapy is on frustrating the individual's usual means of avoidance and encouraging him to bring to awareness, as belonging to the self, all those parts of his personality that are alienated. In the safe, experimental, therapeutic situation, the individual may now identify with his own actual experience and needs, instead of with an image or with others' demands. He does this by re-owning his body, the source of his experience of reality. The individual is encouraged to overcome the programmed calm and security of structured existence, whereby, through the computing intellect, he turns himself into a dead thing and flees from his vital personhood. By aiding the individual to discover and to release his imploded muscular armature, to deepen his breathing by allowing his excitement to flow, and to resensitize his sensory apparatus, in short, to re-own his body, Gestalt therapy facilitates integration. This is a process of recovering lost sensibilities which brings into awareness those biological and instinctual urges and impulses upon which meaningful, creative imagery and effective activity are based and whereby self-completion is achieved. Gestalt therapy's focus on *awareness* is based on the assumption that awareness cures, for only as the person is aware of his needs can or will he mobilize sufficient aggression to make contact with whatever is necessary to fulfill those needs. As Perls says:

> The factor of growth is inherent in every organic being, so that if you remove what prevents growth and integration, it should apply to every animal and human being or whatever is growing. If we conceive of a person as preventing himself, or

allowing society to prevent him, from being wholesome, there are no limitations to therapy.[13]

Since we are primarily feeling and operational rather than rational, Gestalt therapy aims to put us in touch with the ongoing, here-and-now process of sensing and feeling, to teach us to trust intuition, the innate intelligence of the organism, upon the basis of which our learning and knowing and reasoning will become unified and meaningful. In Gestalt therapy, one is encouraged to pay attention to, or to concentrate on, the figure which emerges from the background of organismic activity, and this here-and-now concentration brings about a change in one's perception of events and leaves him with a feeling that he is a continuous flow of processes in an organism-environment unity.

The authentic person *is* an organism-environment unity. Though, as I pointed out earlier, Gestalt therapy prefers to speak of activity at the contact-boundary of the organism-environment field rather than of "inner" and "outer," the latter terms are useful for explaining the conception of the authentic person. If we think of three zones in the organism-environment field, we can explicate them as follows: The *inner zone* is the instinctual, animal, sensory, intuitive zone. This is the zone of the self, wherein the orienting (sensoric) and manipulative or coping (motoric) equipment is found. The authentic person is in direct contact with the *outer zone*, the world of reality, the animate and inanimate environment. In authentic living, the inner and outer zones press against or upon each other. In the purely human sphere, this inner-zone–outer-zone contact or unity equals affiliation or encounter, a genuine and valid human need. When, through tyranny or some other means, such as irreversible and dehumanizing illness (brain damage, for example), the separating

[13] Appendix D, p. 185.

boundaries of individuality are destroyed, confluence or symbiosis results and contact or encounter is no longer possible. Except in moments of ecstasy and self-transcendence, which imply, in order to be authentic, a prior clear sense of self, confluence is the same as the engulfment or possession of the self by alien selves or forces, which characterizes demonic living.

The inauthentic person is in touch with a *middle zone,* instead of with the outer zone. This middle zone is what might be called an assumptive world because it is filled with concepts, images, catastrophic and anastrophic expectations, intellectualizations, rationalizations, and so on, which the individual assumes from others and which he assumes constitute the real world. The middle zone does not derive from awareness of organismic experience; it is as if a chorus, as in Greek tragedy, rather than the self, defines and informs one's existence. The person who lives in the middle zone is not in contact with the environment but with his side of the inner zone, which he presents to the environment as a mask. On the other hand, the environment is not in contact with the authentic self, but with the outside of the middle zone or mask which the individual presents to it. This middle zone shields, protects, and subdues the authentic self, and the person expends his energy in maintaining and developing the mask. The task of Gestalt therapy is to aid the individual, in the safe emergency of the therapeutic situation, to empty out this middle zone so that the contact-boundary of the organism-environment field is restored and the choosing and simultaneous rejecting functions of the ego may proceed on the basis of *felt* experience, which is, of course, the only real experience.[14]

[14] Compare and contrast Gestalt therapy's "inner," "middle," and "outer" zones with Rollo May's treatment of *umwelt* (the natural world including biological needs, drives, instincts), *mitwelt* (the world of inter-

A paranoid woman in her first group therapy meeting on the ward begins by telling in a flat, affectless voice that her husband tried to poison her. She continues to enumerate her delusional complaints, but also mentions a severe pain in the back of her neck. Asked to describe this, she says that it is as though she had been struck a judo blow and also indicates that her husband knows judo. Able now to say that she feels as though her husband had actually struck her, she can, when questioned, soon begin to talk about ways in which her husband symbolically hurt her. Soon she is telling the group, with appropriate tears and anger, how her husband slights and ignores her, and flirts with other women. Temporarily she has abandoned the paranoid solution to her problems.[15]

Gestalt therapy is interested in mere *self-awareness* only as part of the general awareness of the organism-environment field. In other words, the awareness which Gestalt therapy aims for includes, yet is not limited to, self-awareness. Perls asserts that extreme self-awareness leads to hypochrondiasis, to preoccupation with the self, to withdrawal into meditation. If you are too much aware of your self, you miss the world; if you are too much aware of the world, you miss your self. (See Appendix C.) Therefore, in attempting to stress the interdependence of organism and environment, or individual and society, Gestalt therapy considers the formulation of contact-boundary more fundamental than "inner" and "outer," because the concept of contact-boundary overcomes the spurious notion that organism and environment are completely autonomous entities. The intricate relation of the two is such that they are both separate and joined, which is perhaps the *basic* paradox of the many mystifying paradoxes of human existence. In the words of Gestalt therapy: Awareness leads to contact with the "social-animal-physical" field.[16]

---

relationships with human beings), and *eigenwelt* ("own world," the mode least adequately dealt with or understood in modern psychology and depth psychology), in Rollo May *et al.*, *Existence: A New Dimension in Psychiatry* (New York: Basic Books, 1958), pp. 61-65.

[15] John Enright, in Fagan and Shepherd, p. 110.

[16] Perls, *Gestalt Therapy: Excitement and Growth*, p. 228.

Causality, Actuality, and Teleology in Gestalt Therapy

In addition to the simple, operational definition of anxiety as excitement minus sufficient oxygen, Gestalt therapy points out that anxiety is also related to one's way of dealing with the time dimension of existence, with past, present, and future. Anxiety is the gap between the now and the later, the tension between the here-and-now and the there-and-then. Our concerns with causality (past) and teleology (future) make it difficult for us to deal with actuality (present). However, in Gestalt therapy, past and future are differentiations of the present, which is the ever-shifting zero point of time. This relationship can be depicted as follows:

Past   Present   Future

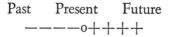

When one is concerned with causality, he moves back into the past; when one is concerned with teleology, he moves forward into the future. Gestalt therapy understands that "the relevant past *is* present here and now, if not in words, then in some bodily tension and attention that can be hopefully brought into awareness." [17] Likewise, the relevant future is present in anticipations, anastrophic and catastrophic expectations, which also are expressed in some bodily tension, if not in words, and which can be brought into awareness and worked through here and now. Hence, anxiety is the cutting off of here-and-now excitement through the deadening or tensing of sensorimotor parts of the self for the purpose of avoiding painful memories (past) and/or expectations (future).

[17] John Enright, in Fagan and Shepherd, p. 123.

Actuality is always in the present. One remembers past events here and now and imagines the future here and now. The authentic person is characterized by a sense of *presence* based on his awareness of, and participation in, *present* actuality. In Gestalt therapy, the relationship of past and future to the present are continually reexamined in the immediate, ongoing, here-and-now process of the self.

> A young woman in a group talks about the poor relationship she had with her father when she was a teen-ager. She mentions a forthcoming visit to her parents' home and expresses the hope that she will be able to break through her father's wall of indifference. Earlier, she had expressed fear of an older man in the group who, she claimed, seemed distant and cold. When asked if anyone in the group reminds her of her father, she surprises the group by rushing across the room into the arms of the older man and weeping. Afterwards, she is able to say that her own wall had made it difficult for her father, as well as for others, to make contact with her. In the actual group situation, light was shed on her memories and she became aware of how to actualize her dreams for the future.

Only the person who lives *in* the present (this is not the same as living *for* the present) can use creatively the lessons of the past and his dreams of the future in the creation of the eternal now. In other words, the past is re-created and the future is being created in each new, present moment. Therefore, to condemn the here-and-now focus as an incentive to license; to irresponsibility; to acting out; and so on, is to plead for the enshrinement of what Kurt Lewin called "irreality" in the guise of searching the past for causes and daydreaming into the future for utopia. When Gestalt therapy speaks of the here-and-now focus, the term focus implies sharp centering as well as blurred edges, as in photography. Thus, Gestalt therapy conceives of the present as the center or zero point, with the past and the future as blurred edges that keep a certain amount of unclarity in the present scene, in the form of tensions, frustrations, needs, memories, daydreams, and so on, which continually emerge from the stream of awareness. Reference to the necessary "amount of unclarity in the present scene" is simply another way of saying that integration is never a once-for-all occurrence in human experience. The excitement of human existence, with all its difficulties and suffering, inheres precisely in life's rhythmic oscillation between poles of balance and imbalance, and I cannot imagine a duller existence than one which achieves *stasis*. It is not inaccurate to say, in fact, that modern existence is characterized by constipation, blockage, stagnation. Mary Schaldenbrand, discussing "Time, the Self, and Hope" writes:

> As act, not fact, the time of authentic existence overcomes alienation in two ways especially: First, it integrates the three temporal dimensions. For this act anticipates the future, retrieves the past, and attends to the present in a single, though diversified, movement. Thereby, it overcomes the dispersion, *the power of fragmentation, which lurks in the "not yet," the "having been," and the "now."* . . . When the self as possibility, history, and actuality is thus unified, its power of presence is immeasurably heightened.[18]

Gestalt therapy's emphasis on the here-and-now is a perspectival conception in which causal and teleological thinking are replaced by, or are included in, "descriptive participation in process." In this conception, life is narrative (as in ancient Israel), continually being embellished and changed by the narrator as new data (experience) emerges. Whenever the flow of experience is interrupted by the individual, the narrative becomes flat and lifeless, for except in sleep or trance the stream is always in flux. The anxious, imploded, or dead-

[18] In *The Future as the Presence of Shared Hope*, ed. Maryellen Muckenhirn (New York: Sheed & Ward, 1968), pp. 117-18.

ened body is not available for experiencing reality, and it may be said that the anxious person sees and sees but does not perceive; hears and hears but does not understand. Having lost contact with essential parts and processes of the self, and being unable to orient to or cope with the environment adequately, the imploded person demands motivation, stimulation, and support from others. The implicit demand of his life is "move me," or "entertain me," or "take care of me."

There is a valid concern to be raised regarding the here-and-now focus. John Enright points out that a radical concentration upon the here-and-now in a purely verbal therapy would be irresponsible and disastrous. However, Gestalt therapy's experiential and experimental therapeutic situation is an "aggressive, systematic, and constant effort to bring the person's *total communication* into his awareness." [19] A participatory, experimental therapy must utilize the full capacities of man for imagination, creativity, and self-expression. A here-and-now focus in any other situation would only increase the person's already heavy burden of confusion and vulnerability and hence his sense of inferiority, impotence, and despair. Verbal expression, so easily distorted, misunderstood, and utilized for avoiding our experience and misleading others, is a very limited means of representing reality. When the total organism is brought into the therapeutic situation, the being-in-the-world of the person can be examined thoroughly, for *the body does not lie;* and, at the same time, the person is freed from the imposition of the therapist's interpretations, which are, at best, speculations (like efforts in panning for gold in the hope of extracting ore).

Gestalt therapy approaches each individual on the basis of the fact that at each moment the person is what he *is*. What

[19] In Fagan and Shepherd, p. 123.

he has been matters now only in the way that the individual chooses to make it matter, and what he will be is being created in the present moment. The only actuality the individual has is the present moment, and the only authenticity he can express is his presence to life. Hazel Barnes says this, in the introduction to her translation of Sartre's *Existential Psychoanalysis,* as follows:

> Man is neither pushed by the past, nor pulled by the future. He is, at each moment, neither what he has been, nor what he will be. According to Sartre, he is free to change the significance of the past for the present and to choose a new mode of expressing himself in living. Each moment demands that man make himself anew by another free choice.[20]

Failure to integrate the self as history, actuality, and possibility is the essence of disordered living.

Layers of Disordered Existence

In accordance with its conceptual formulations, Gestalt therapy posits the five following neurotic or disordered layers of existence: the cliché layer, the roles and games layer, the anti-existence layer, the implosive or death layer, and the explosive layer.[21]

The Cliché Layer

The *cliché layer* consists of the tokens of relationship that we take for granted, such as saying "good morning," shaking hands, and various other forms of limited relationship. It is important to note that these tokens *can* be leads or openings into more meaningful contact. They can be means of orient-

---

[20] (New York: Philosophical Library, 1953), p. 20.
[21] Perls, *Gestalt Therapy Verbatim,* pp. 55-56; or Fagan and Shepherd, pp. 20-22.

ing ourselves, or setting the stage, for deeper relations. Or they can be ways of setting limits to our relationships with particular persons, ways of saying "this is as far as I wish to go with you"; "nice day, isn't it?" "hello, . . . good-bye." Popularized psychology has led to the perpetration of the mistaken idea that we should strive to be intimate (that is, to relate in depth) with every person we meet, in every situation, at every moment. Clichés *can* be useful limit-setters and escape hatches. However, some persons are hung up in the cliché layer, and refuse to risk themselves in authentic encounter even with significant persons, such as spouses, children, and friends. Such persons tend to relate to others even in profoundly moving moments of life, as in grief and high points of love, as if the cliché approach to life derives from the depths of one's existence, as if clichés constitute a special art form of authentic, sincere relationship. However, the disguised attitude of the cliché layer is this: "If I ask how you are, for God's sake, don't tell me!" If we are aware of this fact, and sometimes decide to utilize the cliché approach as a tool for setting limits for or scouting out the possibilities of deeper encounter, then the cliché approach becomes a tool—which one may or may not decide to use—rather than a layer of existence. As a life-style, the cliché is a humbug approach to life.

The Roles and Games Layer

The *roles and games layer* consists of the superficial, social, "as-if" identifications which characterize manipulations of, rather than encounters with, the environment. Using Perls' basic notion of the "top-dog, under-dog" split which exists in all of us, Everett Shostrom has developed a typology of manipulative roles that we all play from time to time: *bully* versus *nice guy; calculator* versus *clinging vine; judge* versus *protec-*

tor; dictator versus *weakling.*[22] Eric Berne and his associates have catalogued numerous *Games People Play.* Yet, roles and games can be useful for ordering or organizing relationships for the purpose of doing certain tasks. Constructively, they serve the same function as habit in the psychic economy. The problem arises when this layer becomes a life-style and we substitute for a "playful" manipulation of the environment a rigid, ponderous, ritualistic manipulation of ourselves and others. We cease "playing" the role and "become" the role. We no longer play seductive, playboy, little lady, and little man; we "become" the seductress, the Don Juan, the frightened or frigid little lady, the timid or impotent little man, the very important person, and so on. We are always onstage, and the real self rarely if ever emerges from behind the mask.

It is useful to realize that the playful attitude is essential to creative participation in life's rhythmic flux. When we participate playfully in life, we not only discover realms of actuality which otherwise would remain hidden; we also create realms of actuality in the act of taking our unique part in life. If, as Buber maintains, each person is wholly unique in that no other can take his part in life, it follows that to smother one's uniqueness under a standardized or patterned or patented role is to cheat the world of the enrichment of reality that occurs when one takes his own part in life, as one enlivens the environment with his unique presence. When we begin to take the role too seriously, we lose the playful attitude and petrify the vitality and liveliness of the self. And as we become progressively deadened in life, we increase our role-playing in order to avoid the underlying emptiness and despair which precipitated destruction of the playful attitude in the first place. We are caught in a vicious circle. Whereas the playful attitude utilizes life-energy in the service of self-

[22] *Man, the Manipulator* (Nashville: Abingdon Press, 1967), pp. 36-39.

completion, serious role-playing requires the utilization of life-energy in vigilant protection and perpetuation of the image. There is no place for spontaneity and risk-taking here, and this process leads to progressive mummification of human personality.

The point is that "as-if" games are pathological only when taken *too* seriously. Understand, however, that "seriousness" is not properly opposed to "playfulness." Playfulness is to be distinguished from fickleness, which implies instability and capriciousness, the inability or unwillingness to take a firm position at any point. In therapy, for example, the fickle person will do everything the therapist suggests, but in such a way as to rob the activity of its life and meaning. Playfulness, on the other hand, implies a fascinating combination of discipline and tinkering that gives seriousness open-ended, doubtful, lighthearted, curious edges that protect it from becoming ponderous, rigid, ritualistic, or priestly.[23] Children have an amazing capacity to play so seriously that they become involved in what they are doing as if it is a matter of life and death (children play *for real*), and as if it demands all the creativity and energy they can muster, yet without losing sight of the fact that "it's just a game."

Gestalt therapy is a "playful" approach to life. In the open-ended, lighthearted, curious, experimental situation which constitutes Gestalt therapy, the individual and the therapist enter playfully into the *work* of discovering the individual's true self. (Note that despite the playful conditions, Gestalt therapy is called "work.") The individual "writes" various scripts between top-dog (self-righteous; bullying; perfectionistic) and under-dog (procrastinating; wheedling; sabotaging) parts of himself; he acts out these scripts; he identifies with his nonverbal communication and playfully "becomes" it in

[23] *See* Paul Pruyser. *A Dynamic Psychology of Religion* (New York: Harper & Row, 1968), p. 330, for an interesting discussion of the word "playful."

order to hear its message (of bribery, timidity, or passive aggressiveness); he enters into his dreams in order to receive their existential messages, and even completes dreams that he interrupted by waking up. Throughout the process, the individual steps into and out of roles, identifying with each only to see how it "fits" or integrates into his feelings, interests, needs, and desires, and then discarding it for other "as-if" games either as they emerge from his stream of awareness or as they are suggested by the therapist. The result is a *progressive regression* to the authentic self which is obscured by the neurotic layer of roles and games.

When we move beyond the roles and games layer, we deal no longer with superficial dimensions but with life-and-death issues, with experience and suffering, which characterize human existence. As I said earlier, roles and games, while themselves impeding or blocking development, also aid in sustaining the individual's avoidance of what he fears is the emptiness of his existence.

If we can see beyond the mask of a clown—which is what one becomes when he plays a role too seriously (that is, as a style of life)—we invariably discover deep despair. Perls asserts that where some people have a self, most people have a void. Having overidentified with the demands of others and having chosen clichés, roles and games that fit an image or concept, the person discovers that his self is undeveloped or nonexistent.

The Anti-Existence Layer

When the role-playing layer has been worked through, the experience of nothingness and emptiness appears. Gestalt therapy calls this the *anti-existence layer* and characterizes it as the stage in which the person is plagued with existential embarrassment. That is, the individual is embarrassed to be what he truly is. Suffering from the absence of what Paul

Tillich called "the courage to be," the person feels more comfortable playing a role than entering fully into the experience of his true self. It is because the individual has based his life on phony manipulations of the environment, on avoiding frustration and searching for security, on playing roles and games, that he experiences regression to the true self as nothingness. He fears that without the role or image he is nothing. Recall that whereas Freud tended to speak of regression negatively, Gestalt therapy conceives of regression as the shedding or emptying of the middle zone, as moving back to the true self.

William Barrett points out that "human moods and reactions to the encounter with Nothingness vary considerably from person to person, and from culture to culture." [24] In contrast to the Taoist's experience of the Great Void as tranquilizing, peaceful, even joyful, Western man, up to his neck in things and objects, and in the business of mastering them and accumulating more, considers any possible encounter with Nothingness as "negative." We are quick to label any talk that even implies nothingness as *nihilism,* and this label is always pronounced with a measure of moral indignation. However, in Gestalt therapy, the Eastern emphasis on no-*thing*-ness is picked up, and the regression to the true self is then conceived as the fertile void, the stepping-off place for growth and development. Here there is process, happening, which though apparently a sterile void when looked upon from without and with fear becomes, when entered into and explored, a fertile void to be filled by the naturalistic and holistic strivings of the self.

On Groundhog Day, a young lady entered my office saying that, like the Groundhog, she felt as if she were in a dark, dirty hole that was filled with black, decaying roots and earth that

[24] William Barrett, *Irrational Man* (New York: Doubleday and Co., 1958), p. 258.

could not grow anything. When directed to *become* the hole and to describe herself as the hole, she discovered that the soil was actually moist and soft; that there were hundreds of tiny, fragile roots which fed larger roots; and that what had appeared to be black, decaying roots were actually filled with nutriment for the beautiful flowers that were growing above the ground. When told to become the flowers, she discovered that they were not real; they were plastic flowers. Life existed in the dark, dirty hole, not in the too-perfect flowers. The apparent *nothing-ness* proved to be *no-thing-ness*. She concluded that through her need to be perfect she had developed an artificial image (a thing) and had stifled thereby the aliveness and potentiality which characterized her underlying true self.

The essence of the anti-existence layer is the *impasse,* the point at which the phony manipulations of the self no longer make sense and one begins to feel stuck and lost. Instead of risking the suffering and pain of the growth process, the person, through the phobic attitude, withdraws from his confusion, chooses to remain immature, and returns to the security of his phony image whereby he receives support from the environment (in the form of flattery, and so on). However, the impasse is the crucial point of growth, and if the individual understands the impasse, enlightenment occurs and growth begins. Herman Hesse has written that "atonement with the world . . . [is] an intoxicating surrender and deep curiosity about the miraculous." [25] In Gestalt therapy, surrender to and curiosity about the impasse leads to the miraculous discovery of fertility and fullness where one feared there was only sterility and emptiness.

It is strange that the Judeo-Christian religion, one of the predominant forces in Western civilization, has formulated a doctrine of *creatio ex nihilo* (creation out of nothing) and a conception of conversion as self-surrender, yet fails to understand regression, nothingness, and crisis positively. The concepts of creative conflict, of rebirth through death, of creative

[25] *Demian* (New York: Harper & Row, 1965), p. 83.

crisis are mostly concepts to us; consequently, we rush in at the slightest indications of pain. We are not satisfied to make the pain bearable, but alleviate it altogether, never stopping to think that we are thereby stopping the birth process. The task of the therapist is to frustrate the individual's usual means of avoidance so that he will stay with the suffering, confusion, and panic that constitute the impasse and to provide only enough support that the individual's true self can be reborn.

The Implosive or Death Layer

A proper balance of frustration and support is essential because surrender to the impasse leads to discovery either of death or of fear of death. This is the *death layer,* and in Gestalt therapy "the death layer has nothing to do with Freud's death instinct." [26] Instead, this death layer represents implosion, contraction, and compression of the sensory-motor parts of the self, resulting in deadness. The most exaggerated example of this is implosion into the fetal position.

Implosion is the way of avoiding excitement and becoming unexcitable. Through implosion an image of rationality and control is maintained, for life-energy, which makes vital, creative living possible, and which is spontaneous, capricious, nonrational, and psychologically explosive (though organically self-limiting), is tied up in psychosomatic symptoms and fanciful preoccupation. As one of my clients put it: "I freeze not only my body, but my mind as well." In other words, implosion not only desensitizes the body; it also desensitizes the mind, making certain things "unthinkable" and closing off possible discovery of new realms of actuality. Open-mindedness is based on the capacity to "get out of your mind and come to your senses." [27] Many people fear opening their

[26] Perls, *Gestalt Therapy Verbatim,* p. 56.
[27] *Ibid.,* p. 50.

minds and letting awareness flow through because they feel incapable of freely choosing how to act upon or to deal with their awareness. They are afraid of being overwhelmed and controlled by external thoughts, ideas, and feelings. If one identifies with his sensations, perceptions, impulses, interests, and desires as his own, he knows that he can freely choose and reject various means of dealing with them. He becomes responsible for what he is and what he does.

The point is that implosion invades every aspect of life. Instead of experiencing himself as a mass of living processes, the imploded person becomes a thing, process become substance, potency becomes impotency, freedom becomes predictability. The action principle, agency, is sacrificed, and the person becomes a passive figure, observing and reporting on his experience as a spectator. Thus, not *I*, but *it*—the faulty memory; the thought that slipped out; the unconscious; the cultural or family background—is responsible for my existence. Such thinking reveals the faulty equation of responsibility with blame. On the contrary, in Gestalt therapy responsibility means primarily the ability to respond (response-ability): to be alive, to be sensitive, to feel. It means "I am I; I have taken and developed in myself what I can be." [28] More accurately, responsibility means "*I am taking and developing* in myself what I am and what I can be," better suggesting the *process*-nature of life. When understood in this way, responsibility means that consequences are not inevitably disintegrative or "bad," as we tend to assume, but are simply results that follow from or with one's feelings, thoughts, and acts. Since, therefore, life is not a static, rationally sequential, consistent substance or event, but a rhythmically oscillating process, to make a mistake in *this* moment need not be seen as ultimate tragedy because the very next

[28] *Ibid.*, p. 100.

moment brings the opportunity for one to create his existence (i.e., himself) anew. When the image is what counts, we utilize our energy to perpetuate it with behavior that is consistent with the image. However, when the self is what matters, we utilize our energy in the service of completeness and self-actualization, and *consistency* here has to do with removing lumps (introjects) in the personality that clog the flow of life-energy and life-process. Stated differently, regarding the self, the task is to become perfectly inconsistent and unpredictable via openness to perpetual change and growth.

The Explosive Layer

Full participation in the death layer is the only way of making contact with the genuine *explosive layer*, which I call the rebirth layer. "To suffer one's death and to be reborn is not easy." [29] The wisdom of the life-and-death, death-and-rebirth motif in practically every religion is its expression of the inevitability of growth, development, change, revelation, conversion, salvation, redemption, satori, oneness with the All, or whatever the process is called that leads to new life, occurring through "death." The old man dies, the new man comes to life; the childish way is put off, one becomes a man; the old order passes, the new way flourishes; chaos and destruction give way to order and creation; death and the grave lose their sting, resurrection occurs; and so on. The focus here is on death-in-life and aliveness-in-life, rather than on what happens following actual death, which does not yield its mystery and is therefore a realm of speculation completely.

Persons who have reported on wholesome psychedelic experiences almost invariably use death-and-rebirth imagery in attempting to express the deep significance of the experience. Perhaps we can say that those individuals whose psychedelic experiences are incomplete, resulting in a sense of disintegra-

[29] *Ibid.*, flyleaf.

tion (psychosis, suicide, and so on), get "arrested" or blocked in the death experience and linger there until they are unblocked, through the intervention of a facilitator, and can move on into the experience of rebirth. Unfortunately, some such persons, for various reasons, never again get beyond being breathing corpses, such as are often found on the back wards of mental hospitals, and mostly because of psychological, rather than psychedelic, experience. Some preliminary research indicates that several persons who have followed a course of progressive mental illness for many years on the back wards of hospitals have responded miraculously to humane treatment programs, have been restored to a sense of wholeness which the experts thought impossible, and have subsequently discussed their degradation experiences in terms of the travail of the soul as it struggles to be reborn. The parallels of psychedelic experiences and psychosis with religious experience—all of which tend to use death-rebirth imagery—demand further inquiry, which is possible now that scientists, psychologists, and theologians/religionists are becoming less afraid of collaborating on salient issues regarding *human* experience.

In Gestalt therapy, full awareness of and participation in the death layer leads to explosion, the linkup with the authentic self. Perls posits four basic kinds of explosion from the death layer: (a) genuine *grief*, which involves working through a loss (through death or other means of separation) which has not been assimilated; (b) *anger*, which results from remobilization of the ego-functions of alienation and identification and puts the individual in touch with his disgust regarding what is unpalatable to him and with his desire for what is palatable (a stage in which ambi-valences are differentiated into clear positives and negatives); (c) *orgasm*, which results from release of implosion in sexually blocked persons; and (d) *joy* (laughter, *joie de vivre*), which results

103

from the awareness of liveliness, uninterrupted excitement, élan vital, and so on. These explosions empty out the middle zone (expectations, fears, resentments, phony guilt, daydreams which do not "embody" reality) and restore contact with the here-and-now process of life. There is no way to circumvent hell if one would discover new life, for even life's darkest moments signal new possibility. In a real sense, life's brightest moments represent the *fulfillment* of possibility, and it is only when crises arise that new possibility is coming into being. Therefore, any attempt to re-create life by avoiding turmoil (even madness of a sort) will result, at best, in pseudo-life, or in artifacts which ultimately cause more suffering than inheres in the process of rebirth, for rigid, artificial living leads to a pompous self-righteousness which both poisons one's own existence and wreaks havoc in the lives of others. The man who martyrs himself in the pursuit of happiness via artificial rather than authentic existence, and who ultimately discovers the meaninglessness of his life, is full of murderous resentment toward others who have not suffered as much as he toward the discovery of their meaninglessness. Such a person is the busybody who through his codes, biases, and good intentions would impose upon others (always "for their own good") the hell of his artificial existence. One of my friends is fond of saying, in regards to such persons: 'If you see someone coming toward you to do you good, run like hell!"

I am not describing here a magical process of growth-through-suffering, nor making a case for the position that one appreciates his life achievements more if he has to struggle for them, a rationalization that is often used by persons who are somewhat sadistically indifferent to the plight of persons victimized by inequality of opportunity. Instead, I am talking about the creative, redemptive process that *belongs* to life. A physician who understood this principle, Dr. Richard Cabot, wrote, "I am more and more amazed at the intelligence, not of the human brain, but of the other organs of the human body." [30] The wise physician knows that he relies only partly on his medical and surgical treatment and primarily upon the healing power of nature. Hence, medicine becomes an art of making it possible for nature to do its work in the best possible conditions. The physician catalyzes nature's work, where possible and necessary. Likewise, psychotherapy is an art in which the therapist relies only partly upon his technique to aid the person in removing the impediments to growth, in the faith that, once this is accomplished, growth will proceed naturally. Like the obstetrician who introduces enough anesthetic to make the cramps bearable but not enough to foil the birth contractions, the therapist provides enough support to encourage the person to risk the pain of growth, and enough frustration of usual means of flight from pain, that the true self can be reborn. In order to perform his art well, the therapist must have resolved his crucifixion religion which lacks a resurrection-rebirth dimension. He must have come to terms, in other words, with his own fears of death and dying. Death is frightening to most of us because we fear that the death-experience cannot be lived through, that suffering must be avoided at all costs. We must be *right* at all times, for example, even if being wrong means that we discover new possibilities for being. This is, of course, the logical conclusion of the pathological-medical-scientific model which is concerned primarily with perpetuating or prolonging, rather than with completing, life. Hence, neither individuals nor groups which enshrine the pathological model will tolerate crisis, turmoil, and challenge. Fortunately, the pathological model is always in tension with the innate striving of the self for integration and growth.

[30] In *The Art of Ministering to the Sick,* by Richard C. Cabot and Russell L. Dicks (New York: The Macmillan Co., 1936), p. 118.

I am not advocating a preoccupation with the dark side of life. Instead, I am encouraging the inclusion in human experience, as "natural," nature's signals of the need for change —conflict, frustration, and pain. In his imaginative, unpaginated autobiography (suggesting the *process* of life), Perls wrote, "It is impossible by the very nature of awareness to be continuously happy. . . . Awareness exists by the very nature of change. . . . To seek pain and make a virtue out of it is one thing, to understand pain and make use of nature's signal is another." [31]

"Coming to Your Senses"

Van Dusen points out that strict adherence to the theory of Gestalt therapy demands a specific therapeutic approach. He writes: ". . . the entrance is phenomenological, the inside of the house [of existential analysis] is ontological, the essential nature of man." [32] Rasa Gustaitis has written that Fritz Perls is more like a guru than like a traditional American psychotherapist. The point is that Gestalt therapy integrates east and west in its emphases on contact and withdrawal, transcendence and immanence, separateness and relatedness, alienation and identification, and so on, which inhere in Gestalt therapy's formulation of *gestalten* formation. Gestalt therapy centers on the ontological, the critical, the here-and-now by examining the person's choosing—including how he chooses to *avoid* his experience. Unlike many approaches to group therapy in which a norm tends to be established by a power elite of dominating, sometimes experienced, group members—which may or may not include the therapist— who then attempt to adjust individuals to that norm, Gestalt

[31] Perls, *In and Out the Garbage Pail* (Lafayette, Calif.: The Real People Press, 1969).
[32] *American Journal of Psychoanalysis*, XX (1960), 36.

therapy explores the pathology of "normality." Gestalt therapy is an approach in which the therapist works with individuals who are dissatisfied with the way they are and who are willing to do the hard work of removing impediments to the growth and development of the authentic, unique self. In Gestalt therapy, which generally occurs in groups, individuals take turns working with the therapist. During this process, others are largely silent, though group members are not prohibited from participating. However, when the group's participation is detrimental to the therapeutic possibilities of an individual's work, as when group members attack the person who is working, or interpret his behavior, or attempt to come to his rescue (with flattery, patronizing support and so on), the therapist intervenes. With the primary encounter existing between the individual and the therapist, who is sensitive to the proper balance of frustration and support, the resistance and avoidance which already characterize the individual's disordered living will not be exacerbated by premature, inauthentic encounter between the individual and other group members. If the assumption is that persons seek aid because they are dissatisfied with their ability to participate in authentic I-Thou encounters, we can no longer assume that authentic encounter will proceed automatically in therapy groups without prior concentration on each unique, individual situation. Groups which proceed, even with the best of intentions (or especially in such cases), merely to make the person over in the predominant image of the group may simply make participants more pliable for whatever persons or systems can bully them into submission.

Gestalt therapy does not secure an *adjustment* and call it a *cure*. However, it should be noted that the Gestalt approach gives the leader a great deal of control-power. It is not inconceivable that a leader with a high need for dominance will use his position in the group to attempt to adjust group

107

members to his own ideals and norms. Theoretically, Gestalt therapy places a great deal of the responsibility for his therapy upon the individual and helps him to achieve that amount of awareness which makes him capable of self-therapy. No matter how theoretically sound it may be, no approach, including Gestalt therapy, is free of the danger of distortion to meet the unwholesome needs of the leader. In fact, my preliminary investigations suggest that many novices are attracted to the Gestalt approach precisely because the spotlight can be so easily focused on the leader, rather than on the process. While granting that aiding the self, and not altering social norms, is the basis of therapy, American therapists generally have fallen into the trap of attempting to adjust "instincts" to prevailing social norms, no matter how little connection these norms have to the individual's experience. In other words, the basic values of society are reflected in both the theory and method of many psychotherapies. Having felt obliged to vindicate conceptual systems which partake of and participate in the biases, fears, and distortions of society, American psychologists are responsible for the development of a body of knowledge which would be very useful to anyone interested in predicting and controlling human personality and behavior, but would only frustrate one who wishes to actualize human potential, or perhaps even to begin to *understand* human potential. Carl Rogers has stated that the science of psychology as it exists today could easily aid in the establishment of a dictatorship through the application of latest psychological procedures, whereas psychology would be disappointing to anyone wishing to democratize his country or to make it more democratic.[33] Rogers attributes this situation to the model of science which psychology has followed that sees, for scientific purposes, a subject, a statistic, with a certain

[33] *Turning On Without Drugs* (New York: The Macmillan Co., 1969), p. 21.

number of traits or responses, rather than a person with a unique potentiality for being. Rogers concludes that the interest in prediction and control helps only a person who wants to control. Gestalt therapy, in its own iconoclastic fashion, rejects the concern with mere adjustment in recognition of the fact that *control* is the problem which precipitates disorder in our lives, whether we are attempting to control others; are being controlled by others; are being controlled by our impulses; or are controlling, rather than expressing, ourselves.

Gestalt therapy, a workshop approach, facilitates the individual's work through various rules and games which put the person in touch with himself. The wisdom of this approach is its acknowledgment of the fact that, in the final analysis, humans are more alike than different and human problems tend largely to be individual variations on major themes. Therefore, if one individual's work with the therapist is effective, each group member derives some benefit, for through identification with salient features of each individual's work each person vicariously works through some of his own problems and removes some of his own blocks. Moreover, through the therapist's facilitation of constructive games, group members learn how to engage in authentic encounter as each becomes a projection screen and feedback agent for the others.

The Development of Aggression

In *Ego, Hunger and Aggression,* Perls points out that Freud's theory of aggression, which is very useful as far as it goes, is faulty because it skips the "biteling" stage of development in the human personality. The stage in which the teeth erupt is when the child secures his first means of attacking his solid environment, in the form of solid food. However, through various means of dental inhibition (of inhibiting biting), the parents damage the child's ability to tackle an object, to aggress toward or against the environment. Eventually, "biting becomes identified with hurting and being hurt," [34] and the individual's capacity to thrust toward existence, to create his world, is squashed.

The development of aggression passes through four stages, as follows: (a) *prenatal*, during which the infant receives sustenance directly from the mother through the placenta; (b) *predental* (suckling), during which the sustenance is liquid, and is secured by the slightly aggressive, though largely automatic, sucking of the child; (c) *incisor* (biteling), during which the destructuring of food begins, through biting (the individual learns to bite off, or choose, his environment; and children also hold the teeth together when they want to reject certain foods); (d) *molar* (biteling and chewling), during which mechanical preparation of food for chemical assimilation by the body occurs. The point is that the stomach is just a skin and is unable to deal with lumps (just as the psyche is unable to deal with introjects; that is, with whole personalities which are "gulped down" without assimilation).

Full development of the aggressive capacities is necessary for wholesome living. When lumps of food are swallowed, gastric juices increase to aid in their destructuring and assimilation, and this is the cause of such difficulties as gastric and duodenal ulcers. When lumps of personalities (such as images, demands, expectations) are swallowed, the innate striving of the self for actualization creates constant tension, ambivalence, and conflict, and this is the cause of disordered living in the emotional-psychological sphere. The use of the teeth, then, is the foremost biological representation of aggression, and because of the structural similarity of mental

[34] Perls, *Ego, Hunger, and Aggression*, p. 108.

110

and physical life, an insufficient use of the front teeth is commensurate with an inability to get a grip on life, to get one's teeth into a task. Levitsky and Perls sum up *Ego, Hunger and Aggression* as follows:

> The title was chosen carefully to carry the message that we must adopt toward psychological and emotional experiences the same active, coping attitudes that we employ in healthy eating. In healthy eating we bite the food; then we effectively chew, grind, and liquefy it. It is then swallowed, digested, metabolized, and assimilated. In this way, we have truly made the food a part of ourselves.[35]

Aggression is the means whereby contact is achieved. Dental inhibition, the prototype of passivity, represents intellectual, emotional, and behavioral absence of wholesome and adequate coping attitudes. Aggression is activity and aliveness; inhibition is passivity and deadness. Hence, in Gestalt therapy, individuals are directed to become aware of their eating habits, of their tendencies to accept without question whatever is given to them, while ignoring the taste, texture, and desirability of their physical *and* mental food. In the process of awareness, the individual discovers how he gulps down his environment, without preparing it for assimilation. A concomitant of this awareness of eating habits is the mobilization of disgust, the vomiting up of introjects, so that what is desirable may be prepared for assimilation and what is undesirable may be rejected. It must be remembered that what is undesirable now may be desirable at some later moment. However, what matters is that one assimilate the now-desirable choice.

Stages, Interventions, Values in Gestalt Therapy

Gestalt therapy proceeds through three generally indistinct and overlapping stages or periods. First, there is the stage of

[35] Fagan and Shepherd, p. 149.

awareness of a permanent stream of consciousness. Second, there is examination of this stream or process of awareness in detail. Third, there is a stage of topological reorientation.[36] In the *sphere of contact*, the third stage aids the individual to recover disowned aspects of himself (projections); to undo psychosomatic (organismic sensorimotor) tensions (retroflections); and to destructure and reassimilate patterns which have been adopted wholesale from others (introjects). In the *sphere of expression*, the emphasis is on the reorganization of language from "it" to "I," as in the following exchange between a therapist and patient:

T: What do you hear in your voice?
P: My voice sounds like it is crying.
T: Can you take responsibility for that by saying, "I am crying?"[37]

When the person has achieved a change in outlook, an adequate technique of self-expression and assimilation; and the ability to extend awareness to the nonverbal level, treatment is finished. The individual can be left to himself because he has achieved that state of integration which facilitates its own development (the principle of organismic self-regulation). Nearing this stage in her therapeutic experience, a female graduate student wrote:

> A snake sheds its skin
>   as it grows;
> I shed mine
>   like a child's puffy snow-clothes.
>
> The wind is cold
>   but I can feel it now;
> Sometime
>   maybe it will be soft and warm.

[36] Frederick S. Perls, "Theory and Technique of Personality Integration," *American Journal of Psychotherapy*, II (1948), 565-86.
[37] Levitsky and Perls, in Fagan and Shepherd, p. 142.

Instead of hoping to cure the person once for all, Gestalt therapy restores the capacity for self-therapy, which was impossible before therapy because the individual systematically avoided the pains and sufferings of the impasse which are the fertilizer of growth.

The interventions of the Gestalt therapist build on actual, present behavior. For example, the therapist might call the person's attention to his posture and direct him simply to *experience* his posture and then to try to put into words the existential meaning of the posture. The therapist frustrates the person in his attempts to avoid his experience in such ways as escaping into memories (past), daydreaming (future), and *talking about* his experiencing. The interventions are almost exclusively "what" and "how" questions, seldom "what for" and "why" (except in the sense of what purpose does this behavior, memory, expectation, and so on, serve for you). As John Enright says, in a discussion of "Gestalt Techniques":

> The questions that introduce these interventions are almost exclusively "what" and "how" questions, seldom "what for" or "why." Most people most of the time don't fully know *what* they are doing, and it is a considerable therapeutic contribution if the patient can achieve a vivid and ongoing awareness of his moment-to-moment behavior and surroundings. In a sense, the achievement of such full awareness is all that therapy need do; when a person feels fully and vividly what he is doing, his concern about why usually fades away. If he does remain interested, he is in a good position to work it out for himself.[38]

When the person has learned to stay in the "continuum of awareness," he learns that his blaming of his suffering on others, his explaining reasons for his behavior, and his defending purposes of his behavior are ways of avoiding responsibility for who and what he is and does, and of seeking

[38] In Fagan and Shepherd, p. 111.

support from others rather than standing on his own. This awareness makes it possible for relevant unfinished situations to be dealt with in the here and now.

Second, therapeutic interventions are ideally and usually noninterpretive. As Ross Snyder says: "The individual is the only person who is in direct contact with what he thinks, feels, experiences." [39] Hence, the aim is for the individual to *discover* what he is doing and thinking and feeling, not for the therapist to observe and *interpret* the person's existence. The therapist creates the conditions in which the person may explore his being-in-the-world, and the therapist facilitates the exploration. The value of concentration and detailed descripton over the search for causes can be illustrated by the "why" game. If to every statement the person makes, the therapist asks "why," the person, after trying to make rational sense out of irrational sensations or processes, will eventually come to a fatalistic answer, such as "the universe works that way," or "that's the way life is." Usually, this will end the game, as the person realizes that there is no final answer to "why" questions and that they are means of maintaining the status quo by avoiding the here and now. However, some persons are so preoccupied with "why" that they will attempt to answer even when asked, "and why is life that way?" To take the why game seriously is to attest to acceptance of the status quo and to rejection of the human capacity to create life afresh in every new moment.

Whereas psychoanalysis assumes that the hidden gestalt must be sought in explorations into the past (excavations in the unconscious), Gestalt therapy assumes that the hidden gestalt (memory or expectation) is so strong that it must show in the foreground, mostly in the shape of a symptom or other disguised expression. For example, a message or attitude may

[39] *Inscape*, p. 39.

be implied by the person's words, postures, and gestures, and the therapist may "feed a sentence" to the person and direct the person to say it to other group members and to add relevant material, to see if it fits the person's experience. Through his active participation, the person *experiences his experience* and assimilates this experience, rather than assimilating *interpretations about* his experience. The therapist, relying on the person's ability to identify with his unaware, alienated activity, frees himself from the need to fit the data to the correct conception or category and hence frees himself to participate in the process, rather than just observe it. The patient is led to *become,* for experimental purposes, his voice, an urge, a fantasy, or an imagined attitude of another person, in the process of which he reowns his alienated parts and processes.

Often the person is asked to reverse what he is saying, feeling, and doing, to take the exactly opposite position. This reversal of attitudes, and so on, leads to the discovery that alienated parts and processes can be integrated into, and can enhance images that have been rigidly overdeveloped in one direction. Integration means, of course, that the image has been changed. Instead of dualities, Gestalt therapy speaks of polarities, which, when clearly and accurately differentiated, lead to integration. For example, *compulsive independence* and *parasitical dependence* integrate as the capacity for *mutual interdependence,* with its natural rhythm of nurturing and being nurtured. Reversal can be applied to physical attitudes as well as to feelings, in the process of which psychological concomitants of physical attitudes are brought to awareness.

In the noninterpretive approach of Gestalt therapy, values are situational; they are a function of the context. Only the situation is in control, in contrast to prior value commitments of either the therapist or the client. The emphasis is upon learning to cope adequately by understanding one's situation and acting according to the needs of the situation. Whatever happens is allowed to emerge, for only when one is fully aware of the possibilities of the situation can a responsible commitment be made. Our capacities for learning, knowing, and acting intuitively are buried under our obsession with "thinking," whereby we attempt to guarantee security before we act, thus robbing life of its creative possibilities and risks. The assertion that we are primarily feeling and operational, rather than verbal, is thus considered pure blasphemy by the average individual, including some therapists. Obviously, in the unity of thought, feeling, and act which characterizes man at his best, a responsible commitment *is* the act which crystallizes the emotion and thought of the self. Stated differently, the only way to determine the value of a thought or feeling is to perform an act that confirms and embodies, or confutes, a particular thought or feeling. Thus, absolute security is impossible in the full human life; the only accurate validation or invalidation of an act is the act itself (including its consequences or results).

Finally, interventions in Gestalt therapy continually operate to enhance and to expand the individual's sense of responsibility for his existence. The main way in which this is done is by changing "it" language to "I" language. "It is frightening" becomes "I am afraid," followed by detailed description of how one is making himself afraid. "It is choking me" becomes "I am killing myself," with scrutiny of how one deadens his life. And so on. Changing "it" to "I" restores a sense of agency, the true meaning of responsibility. Enright asserts that true responsibility in the broader (social) sense is rooted in this feeling of being the actual agent of one's life who makes things happen, rather than the one to whom things happen mysteriously.[40] In addition, the therapist calls

[40] John Enright, in Fagan and Shepherd, p. 111.

116

the individual's attention to avoidance of incisiveness and decisiveness through *qualifications*, such as "I guess" and "maybe." Also, questions are changed into statements, for most questions contain hidden agendas; they seek *support* rather than *information* and contain attacks, criticisms, and demands, for which the individual refuses to take responsibility. By turning questions into statements, the person learns to be self-supporting. By skillfully frustrating avoidance-through-verbal-tricks, the therapist helps people to mature.

Dream Work

Perhaps the most innovative aspect of Gestalt therapy is its dream-work method, which clearly demonstrates the non-interpretive bias of Gestalt therapy. In dream work (not dream analysis) the emphasis is on experiencing the dream in the here and now. The person is directed to narrate the dream in the present tense, as if it were happening now, and to act out the various symbols of the dream, animate and inanimate, which represent alienated, unaware aspects of himself. The dream is then taken as an existential message which crystallizes the person's life situation and which contains clues for changing the nightmare of mummification into dramatic or active participation in the flow of life. In dream work, the disembodied spirit and the disenchanted body are reunited into a vital self as the person identifies with alienated parts of himself in his dramatic production of his dream, in which he plays all the roles.

A restless, domineering, manipulative woman dreamed of walking down a crooked path in a forest of tall straight trees. Asking her to *become* one of the trees makes her feel more serene and deeply rooted. By taking these feelings back into her current life, she then experienced both the lack of them and the possibilities of achieving them. *Becoming* the crooked path, her eyes filled with tears as she experienced more intensely the devious

117

crookedness of her own life, and again, the possibilities of straightening out a little if she chose."[41]

In our culture, blacks and other disprivileged prople are credited with an earthiness and natural rhythm which allegedly makes them better dancers, athletes, and so on. The evidence suggests that these people have maintained (by and large) a close contact with the organismic unity or soul of man which characterizes him as primarily feeling and operational, rather than rational. We know now that through a vapid rationality Western civilization is killing the soul of man (the center of his emotions, feelings, spirit) and turning him into a rational robot that can neither feel deeply nor act effectively. Perhaps the revolution of minority peoples throughout the world will aid in the revival of man's soul, so that the mummies of our culture may be resurrected. (The powers of fragmentation are such that even when earthy minority persons become bourgeois, hence preoccupied with being or appearing rational, they tend to become dead.) Gestalt therapy's formulation of *natural rhythm*, namely organismic self-regulation, is another way of saying that death and rebirth are part of life's ebb and flow and are evinced in the process of *gestalten* formation. In other words, as one need is met, as one incomplete gestalt is completed, another need or incomplete gestalt will emerge. The organismic balance, which is continuously disturbed by its needs and regained through the gratification or elimination of these needs, is the prototype of the cyclical life-death-rebirth process which underlies the continual excitement and challenge of human existence. Ideally, each cycle of frustration-disequilibrium-death results in integration-restoration-rebirth which actualizes heretofore untapped potential of the self.

[41] *Ibid.*, p. 121.

The point is that integration is never finally and ultimately completed. *Life* is an endless cycle of disturbance and balance, of death and rebirth; *anti-life* is sameness, stasis, stagnation. Stated differently, life is characterized by continual change, and this is cause for rejoicing, not mourning. In the words of James Hillman: "When we ask why each analysis comes upon the death experience so often and in such variety, we find, primarily, *death appears in order to make way for transformation.*" [42] I turn now to an explication of how Gestalt therapy sheds new light upon an understanding of the death-rebirth process that is an essential aspect of *religious experience.*

---

[42] *Suicide and the Soul,* p. 67.

Are you willing to be made nothing? dipped into oblivion? If not, you will never really change.—D. H. Lawrence, *Phoenix*

The very time I thought I was lost, My dungeon shook and my chains fell off—American Slave Song

IV
RELIGIOUS EXPERIENCE:
DEATH AND REBIRTH

Irma Shepherd points out that the consequences of successful Gestalt therapy may be that the person, having become authentic as an experiencing, active agent of his existence, will be dissatisfied with conventional, patented goals and relationships, with the sham of much social interaction, and with the deficiencies and destructiveness of many social and cultural forces and institutions. "Simply stated, extensive experience with Gestalt therapy will likely make patients more unfit for or unadjusted to contemporary society."[1] Shepherd goes on to say that these persons may hopefully utilize their awareness to change the world into "a more compassionate and productive milieu in which human beings can develop, work, and enjoy their full humanness." The point is that the decision to undertake the task of Gestalt therapy cannot be made lightly and with impunity, for Gestalt therapy has to do with the discovery of full humanness in a society in which

[1] Irma Shepherd, "Limitations and Cautions in Gestalt Therapy," in Fagan and Shepherd, p. 238.

120

humanness is minimized. Our society has become more bureaucratic and technocratic, with occasional, glib nods to personhood. We are generally more interested in the development of systems and machines than in the development of persons. Even therapeutic tools have become systems, focusing more on adjusting persons to certain conceptions and behavioral patterns than on restoring persons to free participation in life's ongoing process of change and development. If, therefore, through a successful experience with Gestalt therapy, which takes him seriously as a unique potentiality-for-being, a person discovers the meanings of full humanness for himself, he cannot tolerate the violation of humanness without being aware that he is participating in that violation. He will have changed the content of his purely personal agony—or perhaps merely enlarged it—into continual agony over how to participate in the humanization of the world without needlessly martyrizing himself, either morally or actually. In short, "Gestalt therapy may often offer a promise of integration, freedom, and satori that is very difficult to achieve in this culture," [2] for there is very little in this culture which supports the approach to life which Gestalt therapy encourages and makes possible. In a culture in which security, certainty, and guardedness are prized, any approach which heightens as does Gestalt therapy the awareness of tensions, dilemmas, ambiguities, polarities, risks, and ongoing processes is considered dangerous. Such an approach will expose the individual to purely defensive hostility and attack from others and will tempt him, at the same time, to overzealousness about this new approach so that he tends to make it a requirement, a new tyranny. Of course, to be true to the Gestalt approach to life is to realize that it is an *approach*, a *process*, which is to be re-created in each new moment and which is robbed of its life if it is made into a dictum or system of "shoulds."

[2] *Ibid.*

In the same sense that there is tension in the culture between systems and approaches, states and processes, rigid codes and open guidelines, machines and persons, there is also tension in the relationship between religiosity and *religious experience*. It is interesting to note that the dictionary definitions of "religion" and of words derived from religion are heavily weighted with references to systems of belief, worship, ritual conduct, and derived ethical values, while ignoring the etymological roots of "religion" (*religare*) which mean "to bind, to bind back, to bind together; to be concerned; to pay heed; to be diligent" (in the original meaning of *diligent*, "to esteem highly; to select; to choose or set apart"). Perhaps with the background of ancient Israel's understanding of man as a psychophysical self who, able to be fragmented, is an essential unity, and with the onto-phenomenological approach of Gestalt therapy, we are now in a position to deal with religious experience *as a process of personal crisis and change*. The emphasis here is on *experience* (on awareness, feeling, response) which is essential to meaning, indeed to life, for if one is not aware, does not feel, and cannot respond, he is not alive.

In a *Playboy* magazine essay, entitled "The Uses of the Blues," James Baldwin writes:

> There is something monstrous about never having been hurt, never having been made to bleed, never having lost anything, never having gained anything because life is beautiful, and in order to keep it beautiful you're going to stay just the way you are and you're not going to test your theory against all the possibilities outside. America is something like that. *The failure on our part to accept the reality of pain, of anguish, of ambiguity, of death* has turned us into a very peculiar and sometimes monstrous people. It means for one thing, and it's very serious, that *people who have had no experience have no compassion*. . . . You don't know what the river is like or what the ocean is like standing on the shore. You can't know anything

about life and suppose you can get through it clean. The most monstrous people are those who think they are going to. . . . *If you can live in the full knowledge that you are going to die, that you are not going to live forever, . . . if you can live with the reality of death, you can live.* If you can't do it, *if you spend your entire life in flight from death, you are also in flight from life.* . . . People who in some sense know who they are can't change the world always, but they can do something . . . to make life a little more human.[*]

While pain and suffering are not sufficient conditions of growth, real growth cannot occur without a measure of suffering. Each of us is reluctant to give up the comfort and security of what is familiar to us, and only when we are able to question seriously the adequacy of the familiar for "what is" and for "what is coming into being" can we begin to change. As simple as that sounds, we do not find it easy to change who and what we are.

Erich Fromm, among others, contends that whereas theologians and philosophers have been saying for a century that God is dead, what we now confront is the possibility that *man* is dead, transformed into a thing. Through the pathology of normality, the drive to conform, we have succeeded in seriously damaging, if not killing, human creativity and individuality. The stimulus, excitement, faith, and force that infuse man as a body-soul totality have been deadened by anti-life ideologies and requirements. While we are not yet nonexistent, we do not live fully, in the sense that our existence is devoid of meaning and is largely directed by personal and impersonal forces we do not know or understand. Man, the inspirited body who is capable of in-forming or em-bodying his own reality, is now largely a demonic puppet in the

[*] From "The Uses of the Blues" by James Baldwin, which originally appeared in *Playboy* magazine, January 1964, p. 241; copyright © 1963 by HMH Publishing Co., Inc. Emphasis mine.

parade of life. Thus, we escape from the ambiguities of freedom into the spurious certainties of bondage.

Any conception of man, of psychotherapy, or of religious
experience that does not acknowledge the inevitability of
agony in life surely cannot speak authentically of the meaning of life's ecstasy. Furthermore, such a conception merely
creates the conditions for naïve optimism about progress and
salvation, even in the face of clear expressions of man's demonic potential. As long as we live according to the pleasure-
pain principle, as in Freudian psychology, pain can only be
considered bad. However, when we can acknowledge both
good and evil, pleasure and pain as natural aspects of life,
we can begin to see pain as an indication of the need for
change. One cannot really live if he cancels out the possibility
and capacity really to despair of life. As Hillman says, *"Until
we can say no to life, we have not really said yes to it,* but
have only been carried along by its collective stream." [4] In
a discussion of hope, Mary Schaldenbrand writes: "To appear
at all, hope requires a situation where the reality of evil is
felt so profoundly that despair becomes fully possible. For,
when it deserves its name, hope exists as traversing the men-
ace of despair." [5]

In the wholesome growth-experience, we make contact
with the irrational, demonic, monstrous aspects of ourselves.
In such experience, we discover that there is no real hiding
place from these aspects of our reality, for when we disavow
them (when we do not *integrate* them into our rationality)
we become capable of rationalizing the most monstrous
thoughts and acts. Hence, we often assume that our wills, our
values, our chosen destinies have become the manifest will,
values, and destiny of God. On the other hand, when we dis-

[4] *Suicide and the Soul*, p. 64.
[5] In Muckenhirn, p. 127.

124

cover all the polarities and possibilities of existence, then and only then can integration and growth occur. To be aware of and responsible for all that one is and can be is to know the meaning of integrity, unification, and wholeness.

Regression and Progression in the Process of Change

In order to express the regressive and progressive phenomena of change, descriptions of change frequently contain death and rebirth imagery, especially when they deal with a religious experience. In this study, I am not concerned with institutional dogma, religious ideologies, or theologies. Most literature dealing with religion from a psychological viewpoint is either reductionistic or apologetic. My own interest is in religious experience as a specific instance of personal transformation that implies a *drastic change of a former state.* Leon Salzman writes:

> Religious experience, which may be defined in an infinite number of ways, seems frequently to involve cosmic feelings, states of rapture, and "mystical absorption" occurring when a dissociated tendency reaches awareness and threatens the integration of the personality. This may or may not be followed by schizophrenic process.[6]

On the basis of this understanding, Salzman distinguishes two types of conversion (a generic term for change), as follows: (a) the progressive or maturational type, and (b) the regressive or psychopathological type. The characterization of a type depends upon the overt behavior of the individual after the conversion experience. However, though these distinctions are useful for theoretical and discussion purposes, we get into trouble if we conceive of them as mutually ex-

[6] "Types of Religious Conversion," *Pastoral Psychology,* XVI (September 1966), 11.

clusive. In every process of change, as, for example, in the treatment of alcoholism, there is a real sense in which it is necessary for the individual to reach rock bottom in order to find something firm to stand on before progression or maturation can begin. In Gestalt therapy, this finding of "something firm to stand on" is formulated as *regression* to the authentic self, as emptying out the middle zone (of expectations, demands, daydreams, resentments, assumptions) whereby we become dissociated from ourselves and from the outer zone (the real world) and as moving back or regressing to the inner zone (the instinctual, animal, sensory, intuitive zone). One must shed his mask and rediscover his true self before he can experience real development and growth.

Anton Boisen, pioneer of the clinical training movement which trains clergymen in the application of the principles of the behavioral sciences to their work, has written incisively about the process of change, with particular focus on the regressive and progressive aspects of the process. Having suffered a few psychotic experiences, Boisen felt that emotional disturbances serve to purge the self of concealment or avoidance devices which block development. He felt that eruption into awareness of experience which is generally avoided leads to the overturning of the centers of personal energy, which William James—who had his own severe psychological difficulties—considered the essential mark of the conversion experience. The notion that human stress, religious or otherwise, releases exceptional inner power is not, then, an original notion with Boisen. William James made this very clear in *The Varieties of Religious Experience,* in a discussion of the unconscious as a reservoir of inner power which, when allowed into awareness, makes possible the manifestation of unusual potential in an individual's life. In the same way, Viktor E. Frankl, in his *Logotherapy,* has developed the notion that human stress releases exceptional inner power in the form of the peculiar will that distinguishes human beings from other creatures, namely, the will to meaning. In a discussion of his experiences in a Nazi concentration camp and his work with suffering persons, Frankl demonstrates that even, or especially, in crisis and stress the peculiarly human capacity to create and to find meaning can be fulfilled. Ross Snyder writes about human nature:

> Human nature is the most indestructible thing that we know . . . it goes on surviving in the midst of unbelievable difficulties and persecutions. A person is an overpowering will to be, to attain completion, to arrive at destinations.[7]

In this sense, crisis can be looked upon as a time of dangerous opportunity, for there is no guarantee of maturation, regeneration, or progression inherent in crisis. As every physician knows, the critical point is that point at which the person's condition could go either way and when it is difficult to say whether the forces of regeneration or decay will prevail. At this point, the outcome hangs in the balances.

Like Frankl, Anton Boisen conceptualized the process of change in the context of deep personal suffering and degradation. Therefore, he did not conceive of crisis as an automatic guarantee of regeneration, maturation, or progression, for he knew from personal experience, and therefore appreciated, the regressive, degenerative, and disruptive possibilities—and realities—of crisis. Yet, it was the latter aspects of crisis which Boisen saw as foundations of hope. To him, the turmoil represents "a better self, blind and chained and struggling for release." [8] Crisis reveals the creative potential of complete irrationality in which critical judgment is held in abeyance and one's life-experience is allowed to flow and to sweep aside the debris of the phony self in order that the

[7] *Inscape*, p. 38.
[8] *Exploration of the Inner World* (Chicago: Willett, Clark and Co., 1936), p. 37.

"better," authentic self may be carried to new levels of being.

In the Gestalt therapy, "the better self" of which Boisen speaks is the true self, the center, without which the person drifts toward dissolution and destruction. Boisen characterized the "drifters" as those who "make little or no resistance. They do not fight. They do not attempt to turn over a new leaf. They do not try to do anything about it. They merely shut their eyes and drift." [9] Eventually, the world of fantasy and dreams becomes the real world and the person seldom shows any great emotion. The person becomes listless, ineffective, and unable to care for himself, and is eventually hospitalized. The clearest instance of this is the catatonic stupor, which represents a desperate attempt to reorganize the self, and to mold and to hold oneself together, and which is complemented by periodic instances of extreme excitement. Boisen points out that the catatonic attempt at reorganization may either make or break the person permanently. Such acute disturbances may have either of the following outcomes. First, there may be no particular change; the individual may come out of the disturbance and become "normal" again without growing. Second, the results may be definitely destructive; the victory may go to the segmental and regressive tendencies. From the upheaval the individual may move into a condition of progressive disintegration. Third, the individual may reconstruct his life on the basis of delusional misinterpretation. What is called "the assumptive world" (the world of theories, conceptions, fantasies, fears) may become predominant. This is what Gestalt therapy calls the middle zone, which separates the self from the environment. Fourth, the outcome may be one in which the individual moves from the upheaval into a condition of maturation, progression, regeneration. The favorable outcome is contingent upon the following: (a) a

[9] *Ibid.,* p. 28.

strong-enough sense of self-possession in the individual to stave off complete possession by unacceptable, or unaccepted, tendencies; (b) a willingness on the individual's part to seek help and to open up with someone who is competent to give help; (c) a recovery of a sense of belonging in a group—overcoming isolation and loneliness which has been brought about through voluntary solitary confinement—and the restoration of the ecological unity in the human sphere; and (d) a life situation that admits of satisfactory adjustment. Boisen indicates that if the individual is incapable of coping economically or socially (and societal conditions tend to make this inevitable for persons of certain racial, religious, or national backgrounds), or if the individual can neither own nor control his instinctual cravings, the case is hopeless.[10]

The criteria which are set forth by Boisen regarding a favorable outcome of an acute crisis are strikingly similar to the things which I discussed in a section of Chapter 2 regarding Jesus' exorcising of the demons from the Gerasene demoniac. Moreover, the language used by Boisen could very well be used to explicate Gestalt therapy's formulation of the implosive layer of existence in which we pull ourselves together in lieu of working through the emptiness of our phony roles and discovering the true self. Yet, when the proper conditions of frustration (of our usual means of avoidance) and support (of our genuine needs and desires) are established in the therapeutic situation, the no-thing-ness of our authentic self is contacted and we become able, through self-support, to engage in authentic encounter or community. It is, after all, in the body (the flesh, the center of existence) and in community, with life's inherent crises and sufferings, that one grows in awareness of his transcendent and transcending self.

Boisen posited that the primary problem of many psychotic persons whose cases he had studied was the short-circuiting

[10] Ibid., pp. 159-62.

of self-realization. Perls and others point out that, since each person short-circuits the process of realizing, actualizing, or completing his self in some way, we can speak of a "psychotic core" in each of us. However, Boisen tended to mean that instinctual cravings which *should* have been denied and controlled are not resisted and therefore "dissolve" the personality and prevent self-realization. Here we have an insight into Boisen's own difficulties. In his autobiography *Out of the Depths,* Boisen indicates a perpetual struggle with his sexual instinct. Yet, he never writes about the problem explicitly; he couches it in a discussion of his love for and preoccupation with a lady whom he met as a young man. The following is the kind of oblique reference which characterizes his discussion of the sexual facet of his life:

> The doctors did not believe in talking with patients about their symptoms, which they assumed to be rooted in some as yet undiscovered organic difficulty. The longest time I ever got was fifteen minutes during which the very charming young doctor pointed out that one must not hold the reins too tight in dealing with the sex instinct. Nature, he said, must have its way. It was very clear that he had neither understanding nor interest in the religious aspects of my problem.[11]

Boisen is, of course, writing about a time when the organicist point of view held sway in most hospitals. The point is that here is an indication, though meager, of someone's recognition of Boisen's tendency to overcontrol the sexual aspect of himself and therefore to bind the life-energy in preoccupation with this sphere of life. We now know that nature not only *must* have its way, but also *will* have its way, either through expression by free, considered choice (which is what makes us wholesome and human), or through the return of the repressed in unaware, impulsive expression (which is what makes us disordered and demonic). Contrary to advising con-

[11] *Ibid.,* p. 5.

trol of instinctual cravings in the sense in which Boisen tended to mean "control," Gestalt therapy defines human problems as precisely the overcontrol of instinctual and biological cravings (either through desensitizing or deadening sensorimotor aspects of the self, or through ignoring these aspects) because the individual fears that his capacities to choose and to reject his experience (that is, to make free decisions about his existence from moment to moment as situations require) are inadequate. In short, Gestalt therapy feels that the binding of energy in a single mode or a few modes of life—which violates the holistic functioning of the self by neglecting essential aspects of the self—produces confused neuroticism, frigid living, and possibly psychotic experience. This is the experience of all of us to some extent, and to the extent that we neglect essential aspects of our nature we are neurotic, frigid (lifeless), and psychotic.

Boisen tried to make the point that disturbances, turmoil, conflicts, and crises may *either* make or break the person. They are not invariable "evils"; instead, they represent attempts of the self, by regression to the lower levels of mental life, to assimilate certain hitherto unassimilated portions of life experience. In Gestalt language, they represent the self's need to complete unclosed gestalts, to finish unfinished business, in order to get on with the process of living. In Boisen's words, "they represent the deliquescence [melting away or liquefaction] of the old sets and attitudes which make possible new formations." [12] This perspective allows potential and hope where others see only pathology and despair. Suffering is considered as remedial, as the source of hope, and Boisen feels that when hope departs, pain and suffering also leave. It now seems more accurate to say that when one no longer can experience pain and suffering, he cannot hope. If one cannot *feel life,* with its inevitable mixture of joy and pain,

[12] *Ibid.,* p. 54.

he has no experience and therefore no basis for hope. As Baldwin says, the flight from suffering and death is flight from life. And in the words of James Hillman:

> Every turmoil and disorder called neurosis can be seen as a life and death struggle in which the players are masked. What is called death by the neurotic mainly because it is dark and unknown is a new life trying to break through into consciousness; what he calls life because it is familiar is but a dying pattern he tries to keep alive. . . . Without a dying to the world of the old order, there is no place for renewal, because . . . it is illusory to hope that growth is but an additive process requiring neither sacrifice nor death.[18]

We need not limit ourselves, then, to the negative view of suffering. However, if we are to overcome this limitaiton, we must overcome our tendency to confuse "talking about" something with "experiencing" it. For example, we can talk about love and hope at the same time that we relate to ourselves and to others in very loveless ways and with deep expressions of hopelessness. We can talk about evil, but because we do not allow evil a place in the natural order of life, we cannot experience it. Considering evil inimical to our pursuits of happiness, peace, contentment, and security, we are unable to integrate it into our reality.

Reconciliation to Evil in Religious Experience

Maslow points out in his little book *Religions, Values, and Peak-Experiences* that one of the results of the peak-experience is *reconciliation to evil*. Evil is accepted, understood, seen as belonging to, and as a necessary and proper part of, the whole. In the peak-experience, while the world is seen as acceptable and beautiful, good and desirable, such things as disease, pain, anguish, and death are accepted more totally than at other times. "It is as if the peak-experience reconciled

[18] *Suicide and the Soul,* pp. 67-68.

people to the presence of evil in the world." [14] Maslow is not counseling a position of acquiescence, in which one waits in unrealistic hope for a time when evil will vanish entirely with no effort on the individual's part; nor is he counseling a fatalistic quietism ("that's the way life is," "things will always be that way," and so on). Instead, Maslow suggests that the gods can contemplate and encompass the whole of being as good, just, or inevitable, and therefore can see evil as a product of limited or selfish vision or understanding. Hence, the gods are able to feel pity, charity, kindliness, perhaps sadness or amusement, but not blame or condemnation or disappointment or shock. Reconciliation to evil is, then, a way of becoming "godlike" and does not allow us to be dismayed regarding the possibilities of life simply by the occurrence of evil. In fact, it is not inaccurate to say that the peak-experiences (the high, joyful, restorative, integrative moments of life) are moments of *fulfillment* of possibility, whereas moments of crisis and stress (evil, if you will) merely signal, differentiate, and clarify fresh possibilities which are seeking attention and fulfillment.

Along with Boisen, Maslow, and Hillman, such writers as Ronald D. Laing are making the case that psychotic experience, schizoid suicide, and lesser forms of emotional anguish are expressions of a deep unconscious wish that death (symbolic or real) should prove a pathway to rebirth. These degradation experiences can prove to be ways in which the unborn self can be born. The task of the therapist or religious guide is to facilitate the death-experience, to do battle with the reductive proclivities in psychology and religion, to facilitate the rebirth of the true self which strives to be born, rather than a false socialization in which the individual, by social coercion and compliance, receives a *persona*, a concocted-

---

[14]Maslow, *Religions, Values, and Peak-Experiences*, pp. 63-64.

identity. Through socialization-oriented psychotherapies and religions, people learn how to be better neurotics by talking more glibly about the meanings, causes, and labels of their life-styles or behavior, or, in the case of religion, about the "human condition" and the sinful nature of man.

The Idiosyncratic and Private Nature of Religious Experience

Boisen was primarily concerned with demonstrating what he believed to be the essential similarity of religious experience and acute psychotic experience. At another time and place, it might be useful to discuss the relationship between individual religious experience and corporate expressions of religious concern. For now, I will simply quote William James to the effect that the "abstract definitions and logically concatenated adjectives are after-effects, mere secondary accretions upon a mass of religious experiences." [15] This applies as well to the icons and symbols which derive from a mass of religious experiences and which lose their communicative significance when separated from experience and made sacrosanct in and of themselves. Moreover, sacrosanct symbols and icons prevent fresh symbols and icons, based upon present experience, from coming into being. Consequently, worship, ideally a celebration, has been made sterile in our day by the continued use of symbols and icons that do not express present fulfillment and promise. Jung and his associates have taught us, for example, that the dark, the feminine, and the imperfect (elements that have been de-emphasized, where not neglected altogether, in the Judeo-Christian self symbol) are now asserting themselves in Western civilization, and must be included in our symbols if Western man is to achieve

[15] William James, *Collected Essays and Reviews* (New York: Longmans, Green and Co., 1920), pp. 427-28.

integration and thereby avoid meaningless conflict, personal havoc, and impersonal war. Every dogma, creed, and theological concept is based on an original *experience,* and if corporate religious life does not focus on *experience* (the warm, live, "feeling-ful," vibrant presence of each individual and the meaning of his uniquely immediate existence), corporate religious life will be sterile, even at its best. As with the sterile man or woman the frequency of sexual relations and the perfect tecnique will never issue in the creation of new life, so with sterile religious institutions beautiful pageantry and impressive ritual will not renew. (The difference is that the sterile person can derive something of immediately demonstrable meaning and value from the sex act, given the proper conditions.)

I am focusing on religious experience, in the sense of the original meanings of the word "religion" ("to bind, to bind back, to bind together, to pay heed, to be concerned, to choose or set apart," and so on). More specifically, my focus is on the religious experience as a specific instance of personal change. G. Stanley Hall formulated the nature of religious conversion or change as follows:

> As natural, religion seeks to re-establish a lost unity with nature; as ethical, a reunion of conduct with conscience; as theoretical, it is a "re-at-one-ment" with truth; and as feeling, it is the closing in of the highest love with its supreme object.[16]

In the language of Gestalt therapy, this might be restated as follows: religious experience is the process of integrating the self. It seeks to reestablish the organism-environment unity, the ecological unity, of the physical sphere; it aids the individual to achieve self-support, to become a unity of thought,

[16] *Adolescence: Its Psychology* (New York: D. Appleton and Co., 1904), p. 351. See also Robert N. Beck's interesting essay "Hall's Genetic Psychology and Religious Conversion," *Pastoral Psychology,* September 1965, pp. 45-51.

feeling, and act, to become responsible for his existence, and to reestablish unity in the realm of human ecology or relationships; it aids the individual to discover his true self through which he creates his reality and vindicates the authenticity of his experience; it aids the individual in seeing and remaining open to the ongoing process of life, with its many problems and promises. One person, leaving the institutional church following a therapeutic experience based on Berne's transactional analysis, said, when asked why she was rejecting the church: "Maybe God has something to do with decision, and with real relationship, and with responsibility." Other persons felt that if there is a transcendent, personal God who is responsible for creating human beings, he must certainly be concerned with self-affirmation, rather than self-negation which tends to be one of the implied, if not actual, requirements of religious institutions.[17] Authentic religious experience transcends, questions, and possibly (though not necessarily) ignores institutions of religion, for religious experience is self-validating. The burden of proof is on the critic who maintains that the sentiments reported above, of people who discovered new life through a therapeutic experience, do not constitute the fruits of religious experience. (See Appendix D.)

According to Boisen, the upheaval *is* the religious experience, resulting in changes, answers, and ideas which upset and overturn what one's own previous existence would be expected to permit[18] as, for example, in the Damascus Road experience of Saul of Tarsus. This is difficult for us to accept, for it emphasizes the unique, idiosyncratic, peculiarly personal nature of religious experience, rather than what James called the "over-beliefs" of theological and metaphysical assumptions.

[17] Muriel James, "The Use of Structural Analysis in Pastoral Counseling," *Pastoral Psychology*, October 1968, p. 14.
[18] *Exploration of the Inner World*, pp. 114-18, 296.

Allport has pointed out that "the roots of religion are so numerous, the weight of their influence in individual lives so varied, and the forms of rational interpretation so endless that uniformity of product is impossible." [19] Religious experience cannot be understood unless seen in the context of the total economy of the individual's life. Boisen clearly puts the emphasis on the transformation of personality as the end of all religion, rather than on states of feeling or systems of beliefs. Beliefs can serve the same function as habit in psychic economy in that through them we try to organize our experience so that we can go on living in the world of men, a vast, complex world. However, beliefs tend to rigidify and become self-reinforcing, or "functionally autonomous," and new experience is needed to break the pattern, to change the old order, to move one to another realm of being. A renunciation equivalent to the experience of death must occur in order for rebirth to occur. In this perspective, in which the place and meaning of suffering and change is viewed in light of the total economy of persons' lives, we move from the "psychopathology of religion," which characterized the Freudian era, to the "psychology of religion," which, with onto-phenomenological, existential-humanistic concerns, eschews a priori, reductionistic conclusions. In the words of Allport: "A psychology that impedes the understanding of the religious potentialities of man scarcely deserves to be called a logos of the human psyche at all." [20]

Conversion (this generic term for change) may be defined as a psychological event in which there is a major shift in personality *manifestation*. Tiebout writes: "By seeing conversion in a larger framework, I was able for the first time to

[19] Gordon W. Allport, *The Individual and His Religion* (New York: The Macmillan Co., 1950), p. 26.
[20] Gordon W. Allport, *Becoming* (New Haven: Yale University Press, 1955), p. 98.

recognize and to appreciate the existence, nature, and influence of the so-called positive elements of the mental life." [21] Note that these are the words of a psychiatrist, who writes further:

> Religion provides the cultural via media to the attainment of the affirmative outlook upon life. Religion should function so as to permit the budding and flowering of the positive potential which resides in the deep unconscious *to the end that the individual through his own creative life forces may reach free and outgoing expressions of himself.*[22]

This understanding of religion is concerned with religion's essence of spirituality, rather than with its dogma; with its function, rather than with its form. Through our growing understanding and appreciation of the religious (regenerative, restorative, unifying, changing, transformative, ecstatic, transcendent, creative, integrative, imaginative, vital) potentialities of man, we are *moving toward* the realization of what William James called "the moral equivalent of war" (though we are far from the *realization* of such a thing). This moral equivalent of war toward which we are moving is the utilization of our energy and resources to establish the conditions in which human beings can develop, work, and enjoy their full humanness. And this in the growing realization that man is such a complexity of polarities and tensions that he is capable, at best, of only momentary integration, thus negating utopian fantasies and establishing the grounds for authentic hope, for this means that man is characterized by continual development and change from birth to death. Hence, "holding operations" to maintain the status quo are ludicrous; anything beyond securing a measure of stability in order to make risks reasonable merely stifles growth and creativity.

[21] Harry M. Tiebout, "Conversion as a Psychological Phenomenon," *Pastoral Psychology*, April 1951, p. 28.
[22] *Ibid.*, p. 34. Emphasis mine.

Self-Surrender: "Giving in" versus "Giving up"

The striving for integration and growth which is inherent in every organism (and which may now be called *the religious need* of man) involves a struggle at every level of being which leads to new awareness. The solution to this struggle involves resignation or surrender, not in the sense of giving up, but in the sense of giving in, of entering fully into one's experience. This, indeed, is the attitude of faith: the willingness to risk one's self in the hope that one will emerge from the crisis all right. William James summarizes this attitude as follows:

> The way to success, as vouched for by innumerable authentic personal narrations, is by an anti-moralistic method, by [the] surrender. . . . Passivity, not activity; relaxation, not intentness, should be now the rule. Give up the feeling of responsibility, let go your hold, resign the care of your destiny to higher powers, be genuinely indifferent as to what becomes of it all, and you will find that you gain a perfect inward relief. . . . This is the salvation through self-despair, the dying to be truly born, of Lutheran theology, the passage into *nothing*. . . . To get to it, a critical point must usually be passed, a corner turned within one. Something must give way, a native hardness must break down and liquefy; and this event . . . is frequently sudden and automatic, and leaves on the Subject an impression that he has been wrought on by an external power.[23]

Elizabeth Howes has written that the kind of knowledge that results from this ecstatic, self-transcendent, fluid experience of self-surrender that works toward transformation makes clear the secondary nature of concepts, creeds, and dogmas, for "if one has the experience then . . . one does not have to shout the belief."[24] This is a knowledge based on, and val-

[23] *The Varieties of Religious Experience* (New York: Longmans, Green and Co., 1902; New American Library, 1958), pp. 98-99.
[24] "The Contribution of Dr. C. G. Jung to Our Religious Situation and the Contemporary Scene," *Pastoral Psychology*, February 1966, p. 44.

idated by, *total immersion* in one's experience, which leaves
one with the feeling: "I don't have to *believe; I know.*" When
knowledge has this basis, dogmatism—the exclusion of phenomena which we have not ourselves experienced—becomes
ludicrous and purely defensive, and we become more capable
of sharing the notes from our varied, idiosyncratic experience
as an exercise of mutual contact and enrichment, rather than
as evangelistic attempts to convince each other of the absolute
rightness of our separate experience. Concepts are tools whereby we attempt to translate our private experience into com-
municable form, and something is always lost in the translation, for each of us is the only person in direct contact with
our thoughts, feelings, and experiences. Thus, too much talking about an experience robs it of its life and meaning. Poetry,
music, dance, art, and silence or nonverbal communication
remain the best ways of communicating the incommunicable,
the emotional, the irrational, or nonrational. Consequently,
the individual who is always talking about his therapeutic
experience is in some way resisting the process. He either
means to convince others of his psychological bill of health
and hence his superiority to them, or to plead for tolerance
and support on the grounds that he is "working on his problems," or to coerce others into submitting to his "healthy"
view of things. Beware of the person who revels in talking
about experience! The point is that the ability to *talk about*
something is little or no indication of the ability to *experience,*
or feel, it.

"Creative death; creative conflict; creative suffering." We
tend to be frightened by such words. We tend to think that
any indication of the need for change challenges the validity
of all that existed before. One way of avoiding what is actual
and what is potential is by focusing on the past. To raise
the challenge of the need for change is merely to ask whether
the past is adequate for the present and whether the past

helps to create or stifles the future. The healer's task is to help persons to understand such questions.

Perhaps we can clarify this death-rebirth imagery by referring to experiences with psychedelic drugs, such as LSD and psilocybin. The successful or integrative drug experience is said to result in "a kind of psychic death and rebirth into a new, less threatening world." [25] When a psychedelic is ingested, the self's boundaries are expanded; that is, awareness is heightened, sensibilities are sharpened, hitherto unrealized potential is released. The individual is able to identify with the world in extraordinary ways. Persons speak of hearing colors, of seeing sounds, of perceiving the ebb and flow of the life-energy in exciting, and sometimes frightening, ways. If the individual has a clear sense of identity, if he is fairly capable of directing his life through free choices and decisions (if his ego-boundary is strong), he is likely to have a gratifying experience, with esthetic-religious-therapeutic overtones. He "comes down" with the feeling that he will never again be the same as he was before. He has experienced being "wrenched out of himself" and has been renewed thereby. Though there are cases of persons being able to undertake psychedelic experiences alone, it is often necessary and advisable for a guide to be present to provide whatever support is necessary. None of us is so integrated that the possibility of disaster is nonexistent. Hence, when the aim is to expand existing self-boundaries which are clear and strong, to extend the ego-functions of alienation and identification along the further (perhaps unfathomable) reaches of awareness, and when the proper conditions exist, we know that the experience can be rewarding and growth-enhancing; and the connection between religious experience and psychedelic experi-

[25] Sidney Cohen, "The Uncanny Power of the Hallucinogens," in *The Drug Takers: A* Time-Life *Special Report* (New York: Time, Inc., 1965), p. 99.

ence is seen in the repeated appearance of death-and-rebirth imagery in accounts of both types of experience. But for the one whose sense of self is not very clear, whose ego-functions of alienation and identification are not well developed, and who is seeking easy growth, the experience is likely to be disastrous. However, even with this type of person, research indicates that with adequate preparation, proper dosages of the drug, and well-designed, well-guided experimental situations, benefits can also be many and long-term. In the growth experience, the freely flowing, unruly continuum of awareness bursts in upon one's centers of personal energy, and for this reason a guide is a necessary adjunct in the drug, therapeutic, or religious experience, if the individual is not merely engaging in self-destruction. In either case, the result can be as mild as a mild shock upon being surprised and as overwhelming as an extreme psychotic experience. Nevertheless, when one walks the valley of the shadows and comes out all right, when one has wrestled with his personal demons and has overcome, he knows what it means to be free, and is ever after a difficult man to enslave by any form of tyranny. Yet the signal point is that there is no easy road to rebirth, to growth, to renewal. If one would grow, he must risk all that he is and has in order to make contact with life's ever-new possibilities. Hence, if one is seeking a quick "trip" to utopia, without pain and suffering, he merely substitutes the psychedelic crutch for the environmental crutch (the support he derives from others by substituting an "image" for his true self).

Resignation, surrender, ecstatic absorption, self-transcendence, cosmic feelings, mystical phenomena must be regarded as evidence of the vital turning point of personality change. There is an interesting, inexplicable paradox of change, namely, that the more one tries to change, the more difficult change becomes, and when one gives up trying, change occurs. At that moment, one discovers that he is what Carl Rogers calls a congruent being: he has achieved, or come upon, an adequate matching of awareness, experiencing, and communication. Describing this paradoxical phenomenon in the experience of the main character of his novel *The Fall of Valor*, Charles Jackson writes: "John Grandin had always believed he knew himself through and through; when he found that he did not, he knew himself at last." [26] In the language of the Bible, men are continually renewed "out of the depths"; they are "brought low" as a prerequisite to rebirth. From the innermost parts of the self, from the deepest levels of being, new being arises.

Death and Rebirth in Gestalt Therapy

I want to put this in perspective by briefly recapitulating and expanding Gestalt therapy's formulation and handling of the anti-existence, implosive, and explosive layers of disordered living. Gestalt therapy can be defined as a therapeutic process which aids or facilitates *an intrapersonal power* transaction, leading to an overturning of the center of personal energy in the individual and the transformation of the personality through differentiation and integration. In short, Gestalt therapy aids the individual to recover his soul, his center: his emotions, his feelings, his spirit. Consider the following words of Rollo May:

> When biological life itself is the ultimate value—which I have characterized as a deterioration of the American dream—one must hang on at all costs, and what results is a kind of death-in-life, that is, conformism. Conformism is the tendency of the individual to let himself be swallowed up in a sea of collective responses and attitudes. It is the loss of his own awareness, the loss of his potentialities, the loss of whatever characterizes him as a unique being. By this means he temporarily escapes the anxiety of death, the anxiety of "nonbeing," but at the price of

[26] (New York: Popular Library, 1964), p. 169.

forfeiting life, surrendering his own possibilities and sense of existence. As Paul Tillich put it, he gives up *being* because he is afraid of *nonbeing*. It is a surrendering of the meaning of life because he is afraid of death.[27]

These words, though not written by a Gestalt therapist, accurately describe the anti-existence layer of the disordered life. The anti-life individual suffers from the Ten-Commandment mentality, attempting to fit life to categories which presume to cover every possible situation in life. He will not violate or alter the code, even when the situation demands it, and he will not tolerate anyone who does alter or violate *his* codes, or rather those to which he submits. He is remote-controlled by events and authorities; he is pushed and pulled by an uncut umbilicus. Ross Snyder says of him: he cannot or will not present himself to others as he is, or keep his inner speech and his action in the world tuned in to each other, or live for the good he can see, or go for some participating control over some event. Rather, circumstances and society make choices without him.[28] In short, this person looks to others to affirm his right to exist; he is anxious, existentially embarrassed, to be who he is. Consequently, he surrenders his individuality and eventually experiences (existential) guilt over living a lie.

However, it is important to point out that the anti-existence is a layer which we all reach when we try to grow. To the extent that we are all disordered, disintegrated, we have learned to play certain comfortable, safe-though-phony roles and have adopted some images where the self ought to be. So having lost touch with our true self, we invariably reach a point of confusion, uncertainty, fear in the process of change. We would flee back to the security of the familiar, avoid the suffering, and try to discover the true self rationally.

[27] In *Restless Adventure*, ed. Roger Shinn (New York: Charles Scribner's Sons, 1968), p. 204.
[28] *Inscape*, pp. 28-29.

This is the *impasse,* the sick point, the vital turning point in the growth process. It is the place where one, if he will risk it, may do nothing and be "no-thing" in order to start again. If the impasse is avoided by flight into "illness" (conformity, normality) the unborn self is aborted. If, on the other hand, the therapist is able to provide an adequate amount of support to get the person to stay with the crisis, along with adequate frustration of avoidance tendencies, the person contacts or becomes aware of *how* he implodes himself and thereby kills the true self.

As in landing a plane in difficult weather conditions, so discovering the true self is not easy. Often several approaches must be made before pilot and control tower agree to attempt the landing. Likewise, in the process of change, several thrusts often must be made before there is any success. True and lasting growth requires suffering and takes time, and the therapist's task is as delicate as performing major surgery or as executing a masterpiece of art. Hence, the caution against charlatans who, practicing a new form of technology through preoccupation with techniques and thereby attempting to manipulate people into growth, promise quick and easy cures to long-standing problems. The therapist is present as a catalyst who accepts the person as he is, intervenes where necessary, and knows when to stand out of the way. Accepting the other person, guilt and all, the therapist relieves the anxiety just enough to allow the struggle to cease, and, when the struggle ceases, growth begins.

The how of the struggle is *implosion,* which the dictionary defines as "a bursting inwards;—contrasted with explosion." Implosion is defined more specifically, as "compression of air between the closed glottis and the closed oral and nasal passages, as in forming the voiceless stop *p, t, k.*" Gestalt therapy has demonstrated that when a person feels nervous, fearful, or anxious, he is invariably holding his breath and desensitizing his body. In this way, the person cuts off whatever excitement he feels. This tends to become a way of life in a culture which does not tolerate emotionality. Therefore, instead of crying when we experience grief and finishing that situation, we tighten our jaw, tighten the muscles around our eyes, and so on, to keep from "showing our weakness by crying." Instead of expressing our rage, we tighten the appropriate sensorimotor parts of ourselves to keep us from "losing control." Instead of experiencing sexual urges, we rigidify and desensitize our genitalia and erogenous areas (and need more and more artificial means of "turning on"). No amount of deliberate effort will effect real change and alleviation of implosion or deadness. The person must learn to pay attention to the *how* of his deadness, to explore it diligently, to set apart the various aspects of this deadness. Entering fully into this deadness, this death-in-life, fearing that nothing is there but emptiness, the person discovers, wonder of wonders, long-lost excitement, movement, process, energy. He begins to know the potentialities for ecstasy, transcendence, mystic absorption, and so on, which are inherent in his nature. This should be a good lesson to the members of "the helping professions" (behavioral sciences, teaching, ministry), namely, that one must be able to distinguish phony suffering (the "poor me" game) from authentic growth pains; and where the latter or even their promise exist, the therapist, teacher, or religious guide must be willing to allow, even to encourage, persons to suffer, if he is to be a catalyst rather than a neutralizer or retarder in the growth process.

In the final analysis, the death-rebirth process is a lesson in aloneness, our fear of which seems to be based on our unwillingness to come to terms with ourselves. Consequently, we are an extremely social, though not very sociable, people. Aloneness here has to do with individuality. Perls points out that "to grow up means to be alone, and to be alone is the prerequisite for maturity and contact. Loneliness, isolation, is still longing for support." [29] Part of the objection to entering fully into the growth-crisis is that in crisis the lines are drawn very clearly and one must confront every reality of his existence, or must face the reality that *he chooses* not to do so. Even if the person can only acknowledge that he chooses not to grow, he has made a big step toward becoming responsible for his existence. If the "helper" rushes in prematurely to bandage up the wounds, he does not allow the process to purge away the phony layers which stifle the self.

Entering into the death or implosive layer, marked by "the paralysis of opposing forces," yields integration and new birth. The real impasse is the *experience* of being dead. Perls writes:

> It's not pleasant to get in touch with one's death, but there is no other way out than go through that hellgate of mire, that extreme suffering. I don't preach suffering. . . . But I'm willing to invest myself whenever a suffering, an unpleasantness comes up.[30]

He who loses his life shall find it. Implosion yields *explosion,* which puts one in touch with the authentic person, who is capable of experiencing and expressing his emotions. The authentic person has a center, a feelingful, active core, which in-forms his experience and is embodied in his thoughts and actions. The specific explosions (grief, anger, orgasm, joy) represent the energy that has been tied up in role-playing, image-building, conformism, and so on. These explosions represent the completion of unfinished business. Perls points out that Freud coined the term "compulsive repetition" because he thought that the tendency to repeat certain apparently meaningless acts and thoughts leads to petrification and "death instinct." Perls conceives of the continual repetition

[29] Perls, *Gestalt Therapy Verbatim,* p. 154.
[30] *Ibid.,* p. 56.

147

of an act or thought as representing the self's attempt to close a gestalt.[31] In this perspective, repetition compulsion represents life instinct, rather than death instinct, for only when one situation is completed can another emerge and claim attention.

The therapist must be on guard against phony explosions. For example, the tears of a lady who cries about everything must be carefully explored before a decision is made regarding whether, at a particular moment, they express unfinished grief. Likewise, sporadic explosions in some persons merely represent the kind of periodic expression of excitability which we see in the catatonic individual; these are not explosions which have been harnessed by the self and therefore cannot be taken as the kind of genuine explosion that leads to growth and development (the only final tests of an explosion). The authentic explosion represents a melting of the self, or, as James wrote, "the breaking down and liquefying of a . . . hardness." Self-consciousness disappears, and the disruptive overturning of centers of personal energy allows the inrushing of strong sensorimotor impressions. A sense of unity, oneness, wholeness pervades the awareness. One feels at one and the same time his inexplicable separateness from, yet relatedness to, the world, shattering the ordinary illusion of the self and the world as separate and distinct.

Rollo May writes:

The critical issue in the facing of death lies in this area of the human's capacity for self-consciousness. This is true not only in the respect that actual death consists of the blotting out of consciousness, but in the respect that the *experience* of being alive, in contrast to mere *biological* existence, lies in certain qualities of consciousness.[32]

Through one's unique, original consciousness or awareness,

[31] *Ibid.*, p. 90.
[32] Shinn, *Restless Adventure*, p. 206.

he creates his world. His feelings, tastes, ideas, perceptions, values, interests, and so on, derive from the individual's original act of awareness, and out of this awareness he will live and die as a separate person. If there is any question about the priority of separateness, individuality, or aloneness over relatedness, sociality, or unity, the question is wiped out by the fact of death. I can consider the death of another and feel overwhelming grief; yet, the grief I feel at such times cannot begin to compare with the depth of complex feeling which accompanies my consideration of *my* death. The existentialists have made it very clear that we are distinguished from other creatures, so far as we know, by self-awareness and awareness of our potential nonbeing. Suppression of this twofold awareness is suppression also of the potentialities of human existence. (We do not need to belabor the point, that, through a multimillion dollar funeral industry and all kinds of word-magic, we deny the reality of death.) If we can understand and appreciate the continual oscillation of death and rebirth which characterizes the full life, we can discover what it means to live in full humanness. In the process, the specter of actual death will be easier to live with, for we will know that the best preparation for actual death is living the full life, through complete participation in all of its stresses and sufferings, delights and joys.

Perhaps this point will be clarified even further by a focus on the peculiarly spiritual or sacramental nature of the gratifying sexual experience, to which I turn in the following chapter.

> Through sex, one discovers something he can explore in no other way. He is a physical being; and through sex he discovers something of another being, and thus also of himself, that he had not, from the inside, "known" before. . . . Sex is in some basic sense sacramental, in that a spiritual gift has emerged through a physical act.—Seward Hiltner, *Sex and the Christian Life*

V

SEXUALITY AND SPIRITUALITY

Through our overemphasis of socialization, we have succeeded in damaging, if not crushing completely, the *spirit* which characterizes human existence. While socialization is a necessary process of teaching persons to relate to others in the complex situations that develop when even two individualities meet, if the result is that the spiritual essence of life, namely, the instinctual, animal, sensory, intuitive, rhythmic, emotive, vital core of life, is crushed, persons become robots, incapable of authentic participation in life's ebb and flow. In this chapter, I want to enlarge upon the meaning of the spiritual core of life and therefore upon the intricate connections of separateness (agency) and relatedness (communion), of death and rebirth, in the life-process.

In the first chapter, I pointed out the essential connections of spirit and life in ancient Israel, where the word that was used to refer to man as human meant "soul," "spirit," and "breath." *Life* and *death* were references, then, to one's vitality, aliveness, influence, potential, presence, rather than to existence or nonexistence. The absence of these meant that one had lost his soulful-ness; that one's spirit had been damaged or destroyed; and that one's participation in life lacked the breathiness that accompanies or characterizes excitement and excitability. In short, the absence of awareness meant that one was not alive, and awareness grows out of emotions, feelings, perceptions, and so on, which the human being is capable of synthesizing into a peculiar unity of thought, emotion, and action. So in the creation myth man was just a body until he was enlivened by the creator's breath and became a peculiar totality of body and soul, a spirited creature capable of response and responsibility. Our present situation is that we have mummified human personality through the maximizing of automatic functioning. Habit, which serves a useful function in psychic economy by leaving us free to attend to the really vital issues of each moment, has become predominant even in the most emotive, spontaneous spheres of existence. We have programmed ourselves for what we consider respectable responses, and thereby we prevent the appropriate responses (those demanded by the ever-changing situation) from even entering the field of awareness. The cyberneticists are now suggesting that before the end of this century it will be possible and perhaps feasible to program human beings in such a way that they will be able to enjoy a sexual experience, an esthetic experience, and so on, simply by pushing buttons on their chests. While this may sound ludicrous (indeed, it is clear evidence of the demonic potential of presumably "valueless science"), such programming of human nature would be merely one step beyond the present automatic functioning of humans. Despite arguments to the contrary, we are largely manipulated either by instincts, or by authorities. Whereas the authorities would have us use our instincts in the service of established goals or control them in capitulation to the authorities' puppeteering, when we do act on our instincts, the burden of proof is on us to demonstrate that we are not simply rebelling. In either case, we are less than human, for "to make a point of maximizing automatic functioning and minimizing awareness in one's life is to welcome death before its time." [1] If human life is anything, it is aliveness, striving, process, which derive from awareness.

Excitement and Anxiety

Gestalt therapy's simple definition of anxiety, "excitement plus inadequate supply of oxygen") also takes the spirited, breathy, soulful quality of human existence seriously.[2] Gestalt therapy demonstrates that the anxious person interrupts and inhibits his excitement by imploding or narrowing his chest, thereby preventing the body from being energized for activity. (The Latin word for anxiety, *angoustia*, means narrowness.) Through continual avoidance of his experience, the individual eventually becomes unaware of himself and his world. He learns to actualize an image and to ignore his instinctual and biological urges which in-form his true self and em-body his actual experience. When, through the restoration of awareness, the implosion is released and the self is again energized, anxiety subsides. The self is restored to aliveness, striving, process.

The unaware person exists in bewilderment. Being out of touch with himself, he cannot understand all the things which somehow happen to him. He may make innumerable resolutions about how he will structure and design his life, yet they continually fail to effect change or development. He may search frantically for solutions to his questions and puzzlement in books, but he only succeeds in collecting leads

[1] Perls, *Gestalt Therapy: Excitement and Growth,* p. 35.
[2] Perls, *Ego, Hunger and Aggression,* p. 77.

about which his enthusiasm is only short-lived. If he is fortunate, he eventually learns that awareness is the only solution to the mystery with which he wrestles. "Mystery" means literally "the closing of the eyes and the ears and the mouth," implying in its strictest use the incapacity of reason to explain it. From what we now know about human nature, we can expand this strict usage of mystery to include the implication that we can discover or at least clarify its meaning by getting in touch with the source of human experience, namely the body. When one allows the body, through its emotive and spiritual essence, to inform the images upon which meaningful action is based, one's "opening up" or unfolding becomes expressive of an *internal* reality and creative of the *external* actuality. In short, much of what we call mystery is simply evidence of our avoidance of the source of our experience and our denigration of emotionality and vitality in the face of our overvaluation of rationality. The solution is reowning the body. Awareness is discovery, revelation, learning, growth, creativity, orientation, contact, fluency, renewal, aliveness. Avoidance is anxiety, concealment, ignorance, stagnation, impotence, confusion, alienation, deadness. However, even when one is in touch with or aware of his experience, an element of mystification remains following the occurrence of enlightenment. Writing about the therapeutic drama of crisis and change, Hillman asserts: "Dipped into oblivion by this experience, one emerges without knowing precisely what has happened; one knows only that one has been changed." [3] I contend that the gratifying sexual experience can help us to clarify what this means.

Human Sexuality: Agency and Communion

Peter Homans has written: "Human sexuality provides the outstanding moral occasion for the integration of agency and

[3] *Suicide and the Soul*, p. 179.

communion." [4] Having adopted the mind-body dualism of Hellenistic culture, Western man is extremely ambivalent about sexuality. Americans have been called the most sex-obsessed *and* the most sexually inhibited people in the world. Whether or not this is accurate, it is true that we have tended (even the most sophisticated of us) to interpret the "fall" of man in sexual terms and to think of man and woman as opposed to each other. It is important to note that the word *'adam* in the creation myth meant man as human or mankind, as opposed to other creatures, rather than man as male. The myth implies that the woman was created for relational or communal purposes which, while including the sexual relationship, is not limited to sex. After the creator has presented man with every other creature in the search for "a helper fit for him," the woman is created because no suitable companion was found. The implication is that without the woman, man is incomplete; he needs a mate, a companion. When the woman is created, she completes *mankind*, for the male constituted only half of a species. Hence, the female exists so that mutual society, or community, might be cultivated among human beings who share a common nature, yet whose differences make possible the occurrence of mutual enrichment and enhancement. Therefore, the narrowly defined sexual relationship is subservient or secondary to community, to mutuality, to authentic contact between male and female; and authentic contact occurs only when two individualities meet and accept each other. In this perspective, discussion of the superiority of male or female does not seem very meaningful or, for that matter, very interesting. The play on the Hebrew words *ish* and *ishshah* to describe the male and the female, respectively, in the creation myth is maintained in our

---

[4] Peter Homans, "Integrating Agency and Communion," review of *The Duality of Human Existence* by David Bakan (Chicago: Rand McNally & Co., 1966), in *The Christian Scholar*, Spring 1967, p. 75.

words "man" and "woman." Without each other, they are incomplete. Throughout the myth, from the imagery of the female's creation out of the male's rib to their expulsion from the garden, the emphasis is on the interdependence of the male and the female.

We all know the joke that asserts the inferiority of woman because she was created out of the man's rib. The least we must acknowledge is that, since this mythical occurrence, man has not been able to create new human life without the woman's primary participation. Moreover, we now know that masculinity and femininity cannot be considered mutually exclusive, for they are psychological capacities rather than gender attributes; masculinity and femininity are aspects of total humanity which ideally are combined in each human personality. Jung and his associates have shown the consequences of the male's neglecting his feminine shadow and the female's neglecting her masculine shadow. In the parental sphere, for example, the father who is unable to accept his tender, nurturing, affectionate, "feminine" feelings will probably appear aloof to his children, and the mother who cannot accept her assertive, forceful, aggressive, "masculine" feelings will probably appear as overprotective and smothering to the children. The children caught in this vicious circle of conflict and ambiguity regarding activity and passivity will probably develop varying degrees of neurotic conformity and neurotic nonconformity in attempts to adapt to this unwholesome situation. In such a situation a child cannot learn to integrate his capacities for agency and communion. Moreover, in the purely personal sphere, Jungian psychology points out the dangers which arise in middle age from earlier neglect of the *shadows* in male and female, ranging from homosexual panic through philandering, divorce, suicidal despair to actual suicide. Though the price of pathological dichotomizing is extremely high, we continue to sustain in our culture the spurious masculine-feminine dichotomies.

In our culture, sexual feelings are invariably felt by many as unpleasant sensations and excitations that must be either discharged or ignored. If discharged (they likely will be, since the individual is constantly bombarded with sexual stimuli in the mass media), the discharge will probably result in little or no pleasure or satisfaction; hence, the discharge must be repeated over and over. This obsessive expression of sexual need grows out of a stockpiling of unfinished sexual situations, namely, situations that did not allay, through full gratification, the sexual excitation of a particular moment. If the sexual excitations and sensations are suppressed or ignored, the activity which does occur—because the individual has programmed himself to be "normal" and sex is normal for everybody at least periodically—will be either mechanical, low-key, noninvolved (schizoid), or sublimated. In point of fact, the concept of sublimation is inadequate, for the individual does not choose to suppress or repress his sexual need and energy and to make that energy available for use in another sphere of life; rather, he chooses to suppress the *expression* of the sexual need. Despite attempts to deal with libido in the broad sense, Freud did not escape the tendency to speak as if it applied to the narrow definition of sex only. Consequently, he coined the term sublimation to mean that if the individual were not expressing his sexual need, the energy was being used elsewhere. His tendency to confuse the broader realm of sexuality with the narrower realm of sex led Freud to the conclusion that the sexual need is not periodic and organismically regulated, but everpresent and overwhelming in force.

Hence, Freud appeared to counsel control of "libido" through suppression of sexual need and involvement in activities that will enhance the development of civilization. If, however, we understand sexual excitations and sensations as representing unfinished organismic situations that are periodic and organismically regulated, we can deal with sexuality more wholesomely. Moreover, if we understand sexuality (the old term was *libido*) as life energy per se, as the force and stimulus of all existence, the concept of sublimation becomes unnecessary, for whenever the person chooses to engage in activity of any sort he will be drawing on a single energy-pool, namely, the life-force.

As a representation of an unfinished organismic situation, the sexual sensation or need demands attention and closure. In this case, closure might result either from full awareness of the need with appropriate thoughts and images, or, if the proper conditions exist, from full awareness that leads to a gratifying sexual experience. In any case, when closure is effected, organismic self-regulation is such that the next unfinished situation of most significance will emerge. If closure is not achieved, fixation results (or what has been called "repetition compulsion") because life innately strives for completion. I want to point out that organismic self-regulation does not allow the establishment of a frequency norm or set of norms to guide everybody's behavior. The frequency of need will vary immensely from person to person, as Masters and Johnson's research is demonstrating for those who needed research to point this out. Organismic self-regulation means simply that the balance of the life-process is maintained by the continual emergence into awareness of salient needs as prior needs are met.

The Gratifying Sexual Experience

The point is that obsessive sexual preoccupation, which is an indication of inoperation of the principle of organismic self-regulation, must not be confused with or used as a guideline for wholesome sexuality. The gratifying sexual experience is a good paradigm of spirituality because it consists of heightened excitement and stimulation; contact which implies a clear sense of self on the part of the persons involved; a growing sense of diminished self (ecstasy and wholesome confluence, the prerequisite to which is prior contact); breathiness; primitive vocalizations (grunts, groans, sighs "too deep for words"); unity of thought, feeling, and act; explosion and release through orgasm; and a resulting sense of fulfillment, relaxation, and restoration. All of these things, in some basic way, characterize the redeeming, restorative, regenerative, creative learning-therapeutic-religious experience. It is in the gratifying sexual experience that the dualities of mind and body, body and soul, spirit and body become most ludicrous and break down altogether.

In the gratifying sexual experience, embracing is the archetypal moment of contact, and contact is *fulfilled* through embracing. As contact is made, the environment diminishes as a concern, and a good gestalt is achieved. (See Appendix E.) The contact is spontaneous, or "capricious, non-rational, and psychologically explosive (though organically self-limiting)."[5] Completely in touch with his center, the person flows with his emotions, feelings, and spirit into a sense of total relationship with the other and eventually with the world. Two become one, not merely in the sense that their bodies are joined together in such closeness that it is as if nothing else exists, but also in the sense that their beings flow together. Confluence of this type, namely the fusion of two *separate* persons who *will* to be joined together, is wholesome, for it is based upon, rather than antithetical to, prior contact. (Confluence is unwholesome only when it signals the avoidance of or incapacity for contact.) In the gratifying

[5] Perls, *Gestalt Therapy: Excitement and Growth,* p. 337.

sexual experience, confluence is experienced as ecstasy which leads, at the point of orgasm, to a sense of oceanic oneness, of participation in a totality to which the self is normally unaccustomed. The boundaries of the self have been burst, and one feels, as James put it, "wrought upon." Anything goes. That is, nothing is screened out, for rationality is required for the screening process, and in the sexual experience rationality corrupts and diminishes full participation and therefore corrupts and diminishes gratification. Gratifying sex is *presence*, total participation with nothing reserved; it is totally earthy, guttural, and "gutter-al," "primitive," rhythmic, and vibrant. Hence, the sexual experience, if it is to be gratifying, cannot be undertaken rationally, for too much mind-control results in frigidity, impotence, premature ejaculation, and so on. Rationality is antithetical to the self-surrender and self-transcendence which are characteristic of wholesome spiritual experience. One-sided rationality and self-control, unbalanced by emotionality and spontaneity, require that even the most moving (e-motion-al) experiences be programmed in terms of some previously established social norm. This fear of emotionality in our culture is reflected in such repeated admonitions as "don't get excited"; "don't get agitated"; "control yourself." Emotionality, movement, agitation, excitement are the stuff of aliveness. In reply to an admonition that he not get emotional, one of my friends said: "Pay very close attention to me when I get emotional, for emotionality may very well be the stream upon which I float my most lucid content." (See Appendix F.) The authentic emotional act represents the unity of thought, emotion, and action which, because it lacks the ungroundedness, artificiality, and clumsiness of the purely rational act, is gratifying, fulfilling, coherent, and clear, though the ultimate mystery remains.

I am aware of the possibility of romanticizing the life even out of the sexual experience. (See Appendix G.) It is possible, by emphasizing the ecstatic, transcendent, restorative, communal potentialities of the sexual experience, to make sex into something more—or less—than it is. I acknowledge, therefore, that authentic contact can be, and in our culture generally is, avoided even in the sexual experience. The closeness of bodies in the sex act, as in nonsexual social gatherings, does not guarantee the actualization of communion. The sex act is as available for use in human depravity as any other sphere of life, and the motives for participation in the act may be so far separated from agentic capacities of either or both participants as to make communion practically impossible. However, should the strivings of the authentic self effect an overturning of the centers of personal energy, even an experience which begins with all the predominant elements of demonic possession can be redeemed and redeeming (as in the Damascus Road experience of Saul of Tarsus). An oft-cited example of this phenomenon in contemporary literature is the relationship of the prostitute and her customer in which, despite the limitations of the situation, some sense of self-worth and self-renewal can and sometimes does occur. In short, the occurrence of transformation in human experience is still too mysterious to be completely codified and defined in terms of absolute criteria regarding the conditions under which it occurs. As Hillman says, one is dipped ito oblivion by the process of change and emerges without knowing precisely what has happened, except that one has changed.

I have chosen the sexual experience as the paradigm of human spirituality and as a means of clarifying the process of change not only because it exemplifies the momentary experiences of inspiration, integration, and restoration which are necessary for the sustenance of human life and striving, but also because sex is obviously the aspect of human experience about which we continue to be most confused and frustrated. We have not yet fully assimilated the import of Freud's contributions to our understanding of human sexuality. If anything, we have learned from Freud primarily how to sexualize things more effectively for exploitative purposes, as in the selling of inferior or unneeded products (and even of *useful* products); the pushing of inferior literature, mediocre theater, and poor art; and the "selling" of political candidates. In very strange and complex ways our moralism, legalism, and consequent prudery, which have deadened us and turned us into mummies, require the constant bombardment of sexual stimuli and preoccupation to "turn us on."

The point I want to make, then, is that surrender, total participation, and "death," as in the gratifying sexual experience, rather than struggle, avoidance, and "deadness," as in moralism and legalism, constitute the way of rebirth and transformation. We are simply more creative, joyful, growthful, and adequate when we dare to be what we really are than when we struggle to be what we are not.

A Note on the Drug Scene

If considered in the context of the pervasive automatic functioning and deadness of our culture, the drug issue is revealed as part of some persons' attempt to enliven bodies that have been disowned and deadened under the pervasive anti-life, anti-self, anti-sex proclivities of the culture, and to recover and expand lost sensibilities and awareness. In short, drug use can be seen as an attempt to restore the spirit of life that has been ignored or crushed in all of us to some extent. To understand the use and abuse of "hard" drugs as deriving simply from examples set by parents in their dependence on "soft" drugs, such as alcohol, pep pills, and tranquilizers, is to ignore the implications of the language which is used to describe the purposes of drug usage: "turn on," "tune in," "blow one's mind" (break with personal reality), "freak out" (lose mental or emotional control), "get high," "trip out," and so on.[6] Such slogans as "turn on, tune in, drop out" suggest that awareness of certain human potentialities for vitality and aliveness are antithetical to the games that are predominant in the culture (*doing* rather than *being, getting ahead,* even at the expense of *giving up* full humanness). The issue of drug usage is very much a part of the critical issues of aliveness and deadness, of the quality of life in our culture, and some persons choose to use drugs to turn on dead bodies and to energize lethargic lives, if only temporarily.

Drugs become, in this context, tools in the search for expanded awareness in a culture peopled largely by zombies. Moreover, the excitement of the cops-and-robbers game which is part of the drug scene merely enhances for many the meaning and stimulation of drug usage, for though the contact is largely negative, it *is* contact. We all know children who, to keep from being ignored by their parents, will deliberately do things that arouse their parents' wrath and thereby initiate human contact, even if that contact comes in the form of severe physical or emotional punishment. Only a reductive mentality could conceive of such strivings of the self for contact and completion as purely pathological. Always in the process of change and self-completion critical points must be reached where we can do nothing and be no-thing in order that we may start over again; and human beings are astoundingly ingenious in precipitating the occurrence of these critical moments. We have learned to speak so glibly of "growing-pains" that we have lost the full import of the label's meanings. The so-called drug crisis, like any other crisis, cannot be prematurely dissolved by dogmatic pronouncements on the evils and destructiveness of drugs if we

[6] Donald B. Louria, *The Drug Scene* (New York: McGraw-Hill, 1968), pp. 207-10.

are to learn new things about the possible further reaches of human awareness. Neither the positive nor the negative evidence regarding drugs is fully in, and we must not only allow, but also encourage responsible experimentation and research with drugs that will teach us how to improve the quality of existence in our culture.

A Note on "Ecology"

We can understand also both the physical and social (human) ecological crises of Western civilization in the context of the deadness of contemporary man which is created and sustained by spurious dualities and dichotomies: soul, mind, and spirit *versus* body, feeling, and material; rationality *versus* emotionality; human *versus* animal; organism *versus* environment, and so on. Having abstracted certain aspects of our existence from the psychophysical (soul-body) totality, we see ourselves as totally separate and distinct from our environment, and we utilize rationality to justify, in the name of progress and national security, the most irrational destruction of our world through the continuing pollution of earth, air, and water. We do not relate to nature so much as we use it and consider ourselves, in some strange way, above it. In the same sense, we focus on the superficial differences of race, creed, and culture in the human sphere and conclude, at least in practice, that men are perhaps more different than alike. In the human sphere, we take too seriously what Peter Berger called "the social fictions" and thus lose contact with the unitive possibilities of human encounter. The restoration of organism-environment unity in both the physical and social spheres (it can be called the I-Thou unity in the purely human sphere) is contingent upon recovery of the perspective which understands man as a psychophysical totality of earthiness and spirituality who, unless he participates in all his ex-

163

perience as a totality, does not really participate. In other words, unless one can see the instance of contact, whether with another person or with the physical environment, as constituting his utterly significant universe of that moment, in which he participates out of self-respect and respect for the value, meaning, and separateness of the other, the encounter will be inauthentic, hence destructive, in some basic way. In this perspective, every experience and every concern are ultimate, insofar as they are based on the total state of one's existence at the moment. Perls and his associates summarize this perspective as follows:

> The self works for its completion but not its perpetuation. When the process of figure-forming is complete and the experience becomes self-contained and the background vanishes, it becomes immediately obvious that the contact-situation as a whole is just one moment of interaction in the organism-environment field.[7]

Therefore, if one wants to test the quality of his life, he need only scrutinize his choosing in the here-and-now, for his choosing is at every moment a commentary on his state of unity or disunity, his aliveness or deadness (in short, his thrust toward existence). Moreover, such a perspective leaves one free from the curse of the ideal, for the mistake of this moment need not mean final and ultimate tragedy. Insofar as hope is renewed in every moment, this perspective also brings fresh meaning to even the most apparently trivial and routine activities, for every moment brings into focus issues of life and death, of aliveness and deadness, and asks whether one shall stagnate and die, or change and live. The true self is real-ized only in the continual ups and downs of dealing with these issues and answering this question.

[7] Perls, *Gestalt Therapy: Excitement and Growth*, p. 420.

In the next and concluding chapter, I will expand the notion that a holistic conception of man that takes seriously the rhythm of harmony and disharmony, of balance and disturbance, does not allow utopianism or a finalized state of completion or redemption.

People have to grow by frustration. . . . Otherwise they have no incentive to develop their own means and ways of coping with the world.— Fritz Perls, *Gestalt Therapy Verbatim*

Happiness happens and is a transitory stage. . . . It is impossible by the very nature of awareness to be continuously happy. . . . Awareness exists by the very nature of change. If there is sameness, there is nothing to be experienced, nothing to be discovered. In behavioristic language there is no stimulus for happiness. —Fritz Perls, *In and Out the Garbage Pail*

VI
BEYOND UTOPIANISM

We have considered the search of modern man for roots, for a sense of belonging, for a source and center of meaning in his existence. Starting with an explication of a concept of totality, namely *soul*, we discovered in Gestalt therapy a contemporary conceptualization of soul as that center of the human self wherein are rooted the emotionality, spirituality, and essential integrity of thought, feeling, and act of human existence. Hence, man derives his belonging, his security, his hope, his sense of self-possession or self-containment from a feeling of at-home-ness in his body, which roots him in time and space. Yet from the time that a child develops a clear sense of himself as a separate, unique individual, forces, threats, pains, and stresses impinge upon him which would separate him from his roots, adjust him to a norm, and thereby guarantee to him, through the deadening of his imagination and the avoidance of his experience, a spurious security and faith. In this way, the individual, if he capitulates to these forces, sacrifices the human capacity for what Martin Buber felt to be characteristic of depth of mind, namely, the capacity to say "I" to another's "Thou."

Utopianism, American Style

The separation of the individual from his roots results in problems, not the least of which is susceptibility to the peculiar brand of utopianism that operates in our culture, and that has no place in a perspective in which life is seen as process, rather than as stasis. America is, in a very basic sense, an infant country, caught up in a spirit of youthfulness and optimism that tends to require denial of the possibility of utter depravity of even the noblest dreams and intentions. We have not yet assimilated the conquering of our geographical frontiers, and we are now faced with threats and challenges on the human frontier which we are unprepared to face. We continue to believe that through growth, through increasingly efficient and powerful technology, through rational self-control that is abstracted from our total experience, and through legalism, we shall one day achieve the ends of our pursuit of happiness in a perfectly ordered society. In the political sphere, for example, there are measures of this naïve utopianism in both liberal and conservative groups. The conservatives tend to imply that if we can make law enforcement effective, we will see that we have already achieved the perfectly ordered society, if everybody would only be satisfied with his present lot, or try to be like the best (or is it the worst?) of the conservatives. The liberals, on the other hand, tend to imply that through the mere passage of the proper social legislation, we can bring about the perfectly ordered society. At some level of awareness we all know that the rose-colored view of human existence is naïve. Yet we tend to include the realm of evil (suffering, pain, death) in our cosmologies only by explaining evil as punishment for failure to fulfill an a priori system of values and beliefs, or as some inexplicable good will of God.

We are now in a position to admit the realm of evil into full awareness, to acknowledge the mystery which surrounds much of evil, and yet to accept suffering, conflict, frustration, stress, and crisis as signals of the need to change, to grow, to claim our freedom from inhibiting, dehumanizing conditions. Even the full awareness of death can serve to spur us to fulfill the opportunities which each moment of existence presents to us, whereas our elaborate conceptions of life after death merely enslave us in a kind of quietism and repression of life. The point is that while utopian dreams can be and often are the slow leavens of a better order[1] many persons, and sometimes total cultures, come to treat these dreams as if they are reality or will someday become reality in such a way that conflict, suffering, and frustration will be eliminated altogether. Hence, persons work frantically and inflexibly in false hope of fulfilling visions that are based on the awareness of particular moments and that, when adhered to rigidly, blind them to fresh possibilities of the everchanging stream of life. In his autobiography *In and Out the Garbage Pail*, in which the unnumbered pages suggest the continual flow of the stream of life, Perls points out that "it is impossible, by the very nature of awareness, for a person to be continually happy." [2] Yet many of us tend to conclude from the constitu-

[1] William James, *The Varieties of Religious Experience*, p. 279.
[2] Frederick S. Perls, *In and Out the Garbage Pail* (Lafayette, Calif.: The Real People Press, 1969).

tional guarantee of our right to the pursuit of happiness that if we simply try hard enough we will someday reach our own personal promised land which flows continually with milk and honey. If such fantasies issue in realistic and meaningful action in the here and now, namely, action which one is willing to adapt to the changing demands of each momentary situation, well and good; if not, they merely signal the release of the demonic potential in human existence and the beginning of a pilgrimage in the land of irreality. In a discussion of the creative potentialities and necessity of conflict in the growing marital relationship and in life, Gibson Winter writes: "The beginning of a new relationship is not an eternal dose of tranquilizers." [3]

Rollo May points out that while the adjustment category is relevant to psychotherapy for helping a person to become free from the compulsion to defy and rebel against his group, becoming able to love one's fellows and to live productively in community must be based on more profound criteria than adjustment.[4] The sick society, in this perspective, is that society which utilizes the authority that has been delegated to its corporate structures to suppress the development of individual potential, and which demands that persons adjust to automatic ways of functioning, rather than teaching persons how to be open to, and deal creatively with, the ongoing process of life. This kind of society plants and fertilizes the seeds of neuroticism, psychotic disorder, and suicidal despair in some, and spurious faith and naïve hope in others. The current upheaval of our society is making it extremely difficult for us to ignore the sick styles of modern living, which some of us too glibly affirm and others too glibly deny. However,

[3] Gibson Winter, *Love and Conflict* (New York: Doubleday & Co., 1958), p. 117.
[4] Rollo May, "Religion, Psychotherapy, and the Achievement of Selfhood," *Pastoral Psychology*, October 1951, p. 32.

169

nowhere is the striving of man against meaninglessness more apparent than in what I call our current "religious experience vacuum."

The Religious Experience Vacuum

Having been disappointed by institutions of religion in our culture, many persons, young and old, seek experiences which renew, restore, integrate, facilitate, change, stimulate, uplift, and transform, in many ways. Some seek such experiences through drugs; others through metaphysical religions; others through communal living; others through positive-thinking movements; others through radical politics; others through astrology; and still others through various forms of psychotherapy, which is rapidly becoming "the new religion." All of these attempts represent the need of modern man to understand his self-experience in ways that provide some sense of unification and wholeness in a fragmented and fragmenting, stifling world.

In a very interesting article dealing with Gestalt therapy, Erving Polster postulates the social need for new religious experience. By "religious" he means "man's concern with his self-experience, and his quest for unity, support, direction, creativity, and microcosm." [5] Polster points out that Freud's early methods were not suitable to a community-wide process because (1) the rituals, such as free association, were too private; (2) the generation was preoccupied with explanations, and Freud and his associates, though aware of the dangers of overintellectualizing, were nonetheless susceptible to these dangers; and (3) the theory and methods were socially nonactivist and unconcerned with fostering good encounter among members of a group. Polster feels that existential psychotherapy, through the uniting of cause and effect,

[5] Erving Polster, "A Contemporary Psychotherapy," *Psychotherapy: Theory, Research and Practice,* III (February 1966), 3.

the appreciation of symbols for their impact *as creative referents* rather than as mere fronts for specific referents, and the uniting of therapist and client in a two-way encounter by obliterating the special dispensations of the therapist, is able to meet the lasting and compelling human needs for community, self-renewal, morality, microcosm, and symbolizing (which is inherent in human experience). The emphasis here is on contemporaneity in psychotherapy, which means a radical concentration on the here-and-now, I-and-Thou encounter which is the source of authentic values, symbols, feelings, sensations, ideas, perceptions, and total experience. The problem with most institutional religion in our culture is that it neglects the here-and-now process, function, and awareness of the self, which are absolutely essential to meaningful religious experience. Consequently, the "uniquely immediate" is missed and the individual is encouraged to live as if he were either in the past or in the future, rather than to accept himself as presently a peculiar cluster of the culmination of life's past experiences and a promise of things to come.

Whether or not we agree with Polster about the religious potentialities of psychotherapy (and the evidence is overwhelmingly favorable to his view that existential psychotherapy is replacing traditional religion in dealing with the peculiarly human concerns of our time), we cannot avoid the absolute necessity of utilizing what psychology and psychotherapy have taught us about human development, disorder, and change if we wish to understand more fully the human self-experience.

The Task of the Contemporary "Seer"

Hence, we may conceptualize the task of the *seer,* be he therapist, clergyman, teacher, friend, or any fairly well-integrated person, as the art of teaching individuals to make authentic contact with the "uniquely immediate" process of life. He must, through a person-to-person encounter, facilitate awareness of bodily sensations upon which "the higher orders of self-experience" [6] (emotions, values, ideas) are based. He must also be able to design experimental situations which provide new opportunities for acting in a safely structured atmosphere, and he must be respectful of the varied potentialities, peculiarities, and individualities of the human material with which he works, which precludes the long-term efficacy of standardization. As he facilitates the awareness of self-experience, he must be capable of standing out of the way so that the growth process may proceed at the unique, individual pace of particular persons. The seer's task is not to *cure* individuals, which suggests a sense of finality and completion once for all. Rather, his task is to aid individuals to set aright their disordered lives so that they may, on their own resources, learn to reorder their own lives as they confront life's continual process of change and growth, of death and rebirth.

This task requires transcendence of the persistent notion, among both practitioners and critics of the art of counseling and psychotherapy, that each therapeutic approach is relevant for and applicable to only the kinds of persons with whom it was originally developed. For example, psychoanalysis was developed largely in work with persons suffering from sexual repression; client-centered therapy with verbally oriented, more or less "normal" college students; Gestalt therapy with overly socialized, restrained, constricted individuals; and so on. However, we know now that each of us is affected in every sphere of life (sexual, social, vocational) by the pressures that impinge upon us in society. Hence, we are distinguished more by the saliency or specificity of our concerns

[6] *Ibid.*, p. 6.

than by the nature of our problems. Therefore, perhaps the therapeutic ideal of the future will be mutual collaboration among therapists of various "schools" which will make for more balanced therapeutic experiences for those who are dissatisfied with the way they are. One way to meet this challenge is through eclectic training programs for therapists (meaning in this context every one whose task is to combat disordered living—psychologists, psychiatrists, ministers, social workers, teachers, and so on). Perls sees this ideal as being worked out in a Gestalt kibbutz where Kubie's ideal of therapist-teacher-psychologist can be put into effect.[7]

Any good "therapist" knows that a technique is merely a limited tool which cannot be applied willy-nilly to every person with whom he works. In fact, he knows that his tool may not be applicable to some persons at all, or that it may have to be changed so radically that it will be unrecognizable. This does not upset the good therapist, for he sees this as part of the challenge, stimulation, and excitement of his work, and of human possibilities. He realizes that a technique is, at best, an orienting tool; at worst, an article of faith, a dogmatism, which becomes a guaranteed limitation or stumbling-block in the growth-process.

Moreover, the good therapist (or seer) knows that even when his therapeutic approach would be appropriate, there are some persons with whom he cannot work because of the present state of his own soul. At such times, referral is indicated. The person must be put in touch with someone who can work with him wholesomely. Beyond this, a part of the therapeutic task is helping persons to follow the sequence that will eventuate in the greatest benefit for them. For example, it may be necessary for persons to experience the kind of acceptance which is inherent in client-centered therapy

[7] Perls, *In and Out the Garbage Pail.*

173

before they can participate in the more aggressive approach
of Gestalt therapy. The point is that no single tool, approach,
or person can be useful to all persons and with all syndromes.
We simply do not know enough about human nature to claim
the universal applicability of any approach(es). The ultimate
ideal is flexibility, development, and change in every therapeutic approach, every therapist, and hence every person who
seeks therapeutic-growth opportunities.

The seer attempts to remain open to, and therefore to see,
potentialities and possibilities where others have settled into
a comfortable illusion of finality and ultimacy. Out of his
vision the seer creates the conditions in which these potentialities and possibilities may be actualized and realized (made
actual and real). In such a conception nothing (no thing) is
sacred. No system, no institution, no idea, no image is valuable beyond its present usefulness; and, in this conception,
no thing that proves to be useless can be salvaged by any
amount of rationalizing or intellectualizing. One has limited
choices of *style* in this conception, namely, either to stand in
the way of expansion and growth, or to permit it and to help
it occur.

Yet *novelty* is not enough. In the words of Abraham
Heschel:

> The authentic individual is neither an end nor a beginning
> but a link between ages, both memory and expectation. Every
> moment is a new beginning within a continuum of history.
> It is fallacious to segregate a moment and not to sense its
> involvement in both past and future. Humbly the past defers
> to the future, but it refuses to be discarded. Only he who is an
> heir is qualified to be a pioneer.[8]

When tradition (or history) is not the vehicle or springboard
of reconstruction and renewal, it is abused, and becomes the

[8] Abraham J. Heschel, *Who Is Man* (Stanford, Calif.: Stanford
University Press, 1965), p. 99.

chain that binds us in demonic denial of our humanness, rather than the foundation that sustains us and makes our risks creative and not destructive.

Occurring as it does through one's willingness to be continually pushed out of shape by the self's strivings for expansion, development, and renewal (in short, through a death-experience), growth itself is seldom without an accompanying sense of joy and wonder at one's seemingly endless abundance. One's own untapped and undiscovered life is the fount of one's fulfillment. If one wishes to put this into religious language, it can be said as follows: one's own untapped and undeveloped life, which may be discovered or revealed if one pays heed to life's ebb and flow, is the Creator's way of giving himself to or incarnating himself in man completely. Such completeness of creativity and potentiality is too much to be contained in rigid images, inflexible styles, and rational categories; and when the attempt is made to contain this completeness, the self invariably attempts to break out of the containment either through the disorder of neurosis and psychosis, or through the ecstasy of growth.

While the moments of integration, utopian fulfillment, and redemption which we experience from time to time are absolutely essential if we are to escape utter despair in our participation in the life-process, these moments can become sources of disaster if we begin to conceive of them as ultimate and final. In short, once we entertain the illusion of finality and completion as a permanent state, rigor mortis sets in on our lives. In reaction to the mechanistic, reductionistic trends of psychoanalysis which tended to paint a gloomy, pessimistic picture regarding human experience and possibilities, we have seen in such works as those of Carl Rogers an equally unbalanced, almost rose-colored view of man which tended to minimize man's demonic possibilities. However, through existential-humanistic emphases, such as in Gestalt therapy, we are learning, in contemporary psychology and religion, how to integrate the negative and positive perspectives into a more realistic view of man. Out of such a view, perhaps we will be able to establish the conditions of change and growth which, based on objectives that derive from the demands of life's everchanging flow, will help us to realize and actualize what it means to be human.

We must find then through our willingness to know and to enter into dynamic relationship with ourselves and others, across every racial, religious, economic, or national line, events which are miraculous, wondrous, ecstatic for us. Yet even these events are not enough to contain the gift of plenty which is inherent in human nature. For, when the momentary *event* of our meeting with ourselves and with others is finished or completed, and we are in that moment renewed and restored, life is such that even then another challenge, another incomplete event, is coming into being and is calling us beyond where we are now. Paradise lost is regained only momentarily, only long enough for one to get his feet on the ground so that he may push off again. As Abraham Heschel says:

> We are involved in a paradox. Discontent is a feeling of uneasiness which we should seek to overcome. Yet to eradicate discontent is to turn man into a machine. Let us imagine a state in which all goals have been achieved—disease overcome, poverty eliminated, longevity achieved, urban communities established on Mars and other planets, the moon made a part of our empire. Will bliss have been achieved? [9]

The point is not that we should make no attempts to overcome disease, eliminate poverty, lengthen life, and so on, but

[9] *Ibid.,* p. 87.

that we should aim to maintain and fan our discontent with our awareness of possibilities which emerge from the life process. "New insight begins when satisfaction comes to an end, when all that has been seen, said, or done looks like a distortion." [10]

---

[10] *Ibid.*, p. 86.

APPENDIX A _____

JAMES F. T. BUGENTAL, ON
"THE POSSIBILITIES OF HUMAN AWARENESS"

In *The Search for Authenticity: An Existential-Analytic Approach to Psychotherapy* (p. 231), James Bugental writes the following about the possibilities of human awareness:

We can now speculate about the further reaches of awareness that may be potential to us. We have no real survey of the probabilities, but varied kinds of experiences can suggest some possibilities.

The unusual perceptual experiences of the sensory-deprivation subjects, the altered consciousness of those who take the psychedelic preparations, the delirium of the desperately ill, the mystic experiences of religious persons, the dreams of normal sleep, the altered consciousness of those who practice meditation, . . . the peak experiences of those who contemplate scenes of great natural beauty, the reports of remarkable perceptions by practicing yoga or certain of the Gestalt therapy exercises or having "bodily awareness" training—all of these and probably many others; what, if anything, have they in common?

179

I believe that many, if not all, are related. I think the common element is an opening of awareness beyond the bounds of our heavily conditioned, daily perceptual limits. Each person interacts with world in his own way, and thus the marked variety of reported percepts. But each person discovers more of world than he has known before, and thus the striking similarities of many of these percepts.

The attempt to list common features is hazardous at best, but it may be useful to note some of the frequently reported aspects:

an intensified experience of color, form, and movement;

a reduced preoccupation with usual, utilitarian meaning;

a reduced concern with the self;

a heightened recognition of linkages or relatedness where they are not usually expected;

an increase of emotional response;

a feeling of "cosmic consciousness" or "oceanic awareness."

APPENDIX B

JAMES HILLMAN, ON
"MEANINGS OF SOUL"

In *Suicide and the Soul* (pp. 44-46), James Hillman discusses the meanings of *soul* as follows:

Experience and suffering are terms long associated with soul. "Soul," however, is not a scientific term, and it appears very rarely in psychology today, and then usually with inverted commas as if to keep it from infecting its scientifically sterile surround. "Soul" cannot be accurately defined, nor is it respectable in scientific discussion as scientific discussion is now understood. There are many words of this sort which carry meaning, yet which find no place in today's science. It does not mean that the references of these words are not real because scientific method leaves them out. Nor does it mean that scientific method fails because it omits these words which lack operational definition. All methods have their limits; we need but keep clear what belongs where.

To understand "soul" we cannot turn to science for a description.

181

Its meaning is best given by its context, and this context has already been partly stated. The root metaphor of the analyst's point of view is that human behaviour is understandable because it has an inside meaning. The inside meaning is suffered and experienced. It is understood by the analyst through sympathy and insight. All these terms are the everyday empirical language of the analyst and provide the context for and are expressions of the analyst's root metaphor. Other words long associated with the word "soul" amplify it further: mind, spirit, heart, life, warmth, humanness, personality, individuality, intentionality, essence, innermost, purpose, emotion, quality, virtue, morality, sin, wisdom, death, God. A soul is said to be "troubled", "old", "disembodied", "immortal", "lost", "innocent", "inspired". Eyes are said to be "soulful", for the eyes are "the mirror of the soul"; but one can be "soulless" by showing no mercy. Most "primitive" languages have elaborate concepts about animated principles which ethnologists have translated by "soul". For these peoples, from ancient Egyptian to modern Eskimo, "soul" is a highly differentiated idea referring to a reality of great impact. The soul has been imaged as the inner man, and as the inner sister or spouse, the place or voice of God within, as a cosmic force in which all humans, even all things living, participate, as having been given by God and thus divine, as a conscience, as a multiplicity and as a unity in diversity, as a harmony, as a fluid, as fire, as dynamic energy, and so on. One can "search one's soul" and one's soul can be "on trial." There are parables describing possession of the soul by and sale of the soul to the Devil, of temptations of the soul, of the damnation and redemption of the soul, of development of the soul through spiritual disciplines, of journeys of the soul. Attempts have been made to localise the soul in specific body organs and regions, to trace its origin to the sperm or egg, to divide it into animal, vegetable, and mineral components, while the search for the soul leads always into the "depths".

As well, arguments continue on the connection of the soul with the body: that they are parallel; that the soul is epiphenomenon of the body, a sort of internal secretion; that the body is only the throbbing visibility of an immaterial form-giving soul; that their relation is irrational and synchronistic, coming and going, fading and waxing, in accordance with psychoid constellations; that there is no relation at all; that the flesh is mortal and the soul eternal, reincarnating by karma through the aeons; that each soul is individual and perishable, while it is the body as matter which cannot be destroyed; that soul is only present in sentient bodies possible of consciousness; or, that souls, like monads, are present in all bodies as the psychic hierarchy of nature alive.

182

From the points of view of logic, theology, and science, these statements are to be proved and disputed. From the point of view of psychology, *they are one and all true positions, in that they are statements about the soul made by the soul.* They are the soul's description of itself in the language of thought (just as the soul images itself in contradictions and paradoxes in the language of poetry and painting). This implies that at different moments each of these statements reflects a phase of the body-soul relationship. . . . We must then conclude that such statements about the soul reflect the state of soul of the one making the statement. They reveal the special bent of a person's own psyche-soma problem, a problem that seems unendingly bound up with psychology and the riddle of the soul, since it is this question—what have the body and soul to do with each other—that the soul is continually putting to us in philosophy, religion, art, and above all in the trials of daily life and death.

APPENDIX C ———————————

AUTHOR'S INTERVIEW WITH
FREDERICK S. PERLS

This is an excerpt from an interview which I conducted with F. S. Perls at Esalen Institute, Big Sur, California, March 16, 1968:

WALKER (hereafter W): You indicate that self-awareness is the basic objective of Gestalt therapy.

PERLS (hereafter P): No. *Awareness* is the basic objective; awareness of our basic needs, not self-awareness. Self-awareness leads to meditation and hypochondriasis. There's always the question of what is the person in touch with. If you're only in touch with yourself, you miss the world. If you're only in touch with the world, you miss your self so that "ecological unity" cannot be established.

W: So in the workshop you are attempting to make the individual who happens to be working with you at the moment aware of everything that's going on in his environment.

P: I don't make him aware, but I find out what he's in touch with and essentially what is missing from his awareness, what he is avoiding, because avoidance leads to holes in the personality. I try to find out where a person is incomplete.

W: What conditions, then, do you create in a workshop in order to bring about the kind of awareness which Gestalt therapy helps persons to achieve?

P: I can only say one thing: by being real, being myself. If a person does not want to work, I'm not interested. I tell the person, for instance, "I'm not interested in being made a fool of by you. Get off the chair; I don't need you." Then very often (this happened in two cases just last week), after being rejected, persons come back and work very effectively. The basic responsibility of the therapist is to be real, to be himself. If he cannot do that, then he cannot help others to become real.

W: Do you see Gestalt therapy as a sure way of shortening the process of psychotherapy?

P: I go even a step further. Of course, I might blow my own trumpet. I see Gestalt therapy so far as the only extant therapy that is effective, which means all the talk about shortening therapy is redundant because if a therapy is not effective it will, like psychoanalysis, go on forever and ever and ever. Take a picture puzzle, for example; you can cut up the pieces more and more and more, but, if you integrate the pieces, eventually the whole picture will be finished.

W: It seems to me that Gestalt therapy, unlike other therapies, is amenable to use with all groups, no matter what their socioeconomic status or verbal facility. Would you comment on that?

P: Well, I would say that the factor of growth is inherent in every organic being, so that if you remove what prevents growth and integration, it should apply to every animal and human being or whatever is growing. If we conceive of a person as preventing himself, or allowing society to prevent him, from being wholesome, there are no limitations to therapy. As a matter of fact, Gestalt therapy now extends towards two sides. On the one hand, even official psychiatry is beginning to accept it, and it has been very reluctant to do so. On the other hand, Gestalt therapy is going into the whole field of education. And one

person I would especially like you to see about in this regard
is Janet Lederman. She did a beautiful work with dropouts,
very disturbed children, using Gestalt therapy in changing extreme antisocial behavior into social behavior, helping children
to find themselves.

W: So the techniques of Gesalt therapy are available for work not
only in the strict therapeutic setting, but also in application to
educational and social problems.

P: I object to the word technique. I don't accept any person as a
competent Gestalt therapist as long as he still uses "techniques."
If he hasn't found his own style, if he doesn't bring himself
across and invent the *means-whereby* (or technique) at the spur
of the moment that is required by the situation, then he is not a
Gestalt therapist. He is an artisan, but not an artist. He is, at
worst, a copycat of Fritz or somebody else, but he is not himself.

W: What do you see as some of the limitations of Gestalt therapy?

P: It's mostly time-involvement. A person comes to a workshop. He
achieves a certain amount of maturation. He has learned to take
certain risks in the supportive environment provided by the
workshop. Then he goes out again into the world, into a strange,
sometimes hostile, environment, and much of what he has
achieved will not last. In general, I would say he makes three
steps forward and one or two steps backward. So what I vis-
ualize as the eventual, let's call it "most likely perfect" therapy,
is a Gestalt community where people go for three or four weeks.
They will work there, live there exclusively until they have
achieved a degree of maturation and reality that will aid them
in tolerating and coping with their average environment and
will help them to start adjusting the environment to their richer
and fuller approach.

W: So that they would perhaps not need to come back for any
special form of therapy ever again.

P: That's right. . . . You see, the word "therapy" is actually not
quite correct anymore because what we deal with is not so much
illness as disorder. Illness is *one* form of inability to cope with
the world.

W: Would you say more about skillfully frustrating persons?

P: Yes. I sometimes say to persons, "You don't want to work. You
want to make a sucker out of me. Get off the chair." I let them

know that if they want to work, I am available to *work with* them, not to *help* them. I think this is the important point where we are now in Gestalt therapy—the realization of the impasse, the blue-baby impasse where a person is stuck with the belief that he can't cope with the situation on his own. He feels he needs environmental support. So, to get a person through that impasse, to make him realize that he can do things for himself against the conviction that he is impotent, the therapist must frustrate the person's usual means of avoiding his experience.

W: Are there any persons, then, with whom Gestalt therapy cannot be used in its present stage of development?

P: I cannot tell you that. I can tell you this much: I believe I personally can cope with any neurosis. I coped successfully with a number of borderline cases. I would say even more than borderline cases. Now, there is something afoot to see if we can go further. We are going to open up a "blow-out" center for schizophrenia, and I'm supposed to do the training for the staff. I hope that next year I can devote my time to research, to see whether we can solve the problem of schizophrenia. I know that those who work with schizophrenic patients talk about much better success when using Gestalt therapy. However, the whole thing is that we are now in the development stages. We are getting at neurotic disturbances where there is still a certain amount of rationality left to the person. We do not know about the deeper disturbed persons, the schizophrenics.

W: How do you compare Gestalt therapy to psychoanalysis? Have you thrown over psychoanalysis completely in your own work?

P: Not completely. I more and more begin to understand Freud, perhaps more than he understood himself. I've been a training analyst in the Freudian school. I have full training in psychoanalysis. There are many half-truths which Freud discovered. Taking the first step in a new direction is so difficult and means so much that people failed to understand that Freud's illness and deep phobia greatly interfered with his solving the neurosis question. The main example I like to give is that Freud himself explained that he could not stand having people stare at him, so he put them on a couch to avoid the encounter. Freud's symptom became the trademark of psychoanalysis, so all the psychoanalysts avoid the human encounter and adhere to the many taboos of analysis. Not only this, but every real thing that happens between the analyst and the patient is explained away

187

by the past and by transference. The result is that you can analyze and analyze and analyze; and Freud himself recognized at the end of his life that an analysis never can be finished. Therefore, I emphasize again and again that Gestalt therapy is an integrative approach, not an analytical one. I've said it before and I say it again and again and again; and this is so difficult to understand: that in our time, our electronic time, we deal with structures, with orientation to *how* a thing works and we leave the mentality of causality, of *why*, behind. Here again, Freud himself has seen that every event is overdetermined, but then at other moments he forgets this and looks for a cause. It's very interesting that I haven't seen any so-called causes, child traumata, that were not inventions of the patient. Perhaps you read this book by Hannah Green, *I Never Promised You a Rose Garden*. There you have it. A beautiful therapist, Frieda Fromm-Reichmann (who actually came from the same Frankfurt school from which I came), discovered that the "trauma" never actually occurred. It was needed to save the self-esteem of the person.

W: You see yourself, then, as completing the half-truths which Freud began?

P: Yes, you might say that. To give you a typical example: Freud discovered the Top-Dog, the superego, but he never realized that the Top-Dog is opposed by an Under-Dog which is just as much striving for control as the Top-Dog. The fact is that the Under-Dog usually wins, through sabotaging (playing stupid, procrastinating, feigning weakness, and so on). The conflict between Top-Dog and Under-Dog is eternalized until they are integrated and the person stands for his own rights, instead of working with or against *shouldism*. When Top-Dog and Under-Dog are integrated, the person knows what *he* wants.

W: What would you say are the challenges of Gestalt therapy for theology or religion in general?

P: Well, that's a very difficult question. Let's start from this point of view: My fantasy about the universe is that it is a process of awareness, which is expressed in theology by attributing to God *infinity, eternity,* and *omniscience.* In other words I believe that the universe has *extension, duration,* and *awareness.* Now, this idea of the universe or matter having awareness has already been mentioned by Berkeley and Whitehead, and we realize more and more that even plants (and eventually we go over to cells) have some awareness; they are aware of what's going on and what they need. There are some beautiful examples of this already. For example, you can take a plant and put some fertilizer in one spot and the plant's roots will grow toward the fertilizer; if you put the fertilizer elsewhere, the plant bends its roots out of a sense of its needs. You know the term *tropism;* and you've probably heard of rats being fed the brain of a rat that had learned to solve the riddle of a maze and then solving the maze very easily because the brain matter contains the information or awareness that is needed.

All we can say about religion: We definitely know that— well, let me put it this way: I see the rise and decline of the U.S.A. and there is hardly any place where you don't see this decline. Where the decline is very much visible is in the deterioration of the church. Now, man needs an orientation, a *weltanschauung,* in regard to the world, and you know how much communism provides people with an orientation which the religious orientation does not have. Now, philosophy in general is too anemic to provide enough of the emotional side of the human being. Political ideologies can provide a tremendous amount of zest and enthusiasm. What Gestalt therapy will do, I don't know. I know that Gestalt therapy is a system of philosophy that covers all possible events and puts the human being (like any other existential philosophy) right into the center of his own being. To what degree it will be able to cope with the projections of the human, with the need for having some responsible directions by God or authority-figures, I don't know.

W: However, it is my feeling that Gestalt therapy does provide religious institutions with clear ways of helping persons to become aware of their projections.

P: Yes. You see, it's very interesting that the German word for minister is *seelesorge,* the healer for the souls. More and more, ministers begin to put their emphasis on being more in touch with their clientele and taking care of them, instead of upon collective preaching. More and more ministers also begin to disown the personalized God and to embrace, let's say, the Jewish idea of God as the unspeakable, the basic creative energy of the universe.

APPENDIX D

ABRAHAM MASLOW, ON
"PERSONAL RELIGIOUS EXPERIENCE"

Regarding the relationship of "religious experience" to institutional expressions of religious concern, Abraham Maslow, in *Religions, Values, and Peak-Experiences* (pp. 27-29), has the following to say:

In effect what I have been saying is that the evidence from the peak-experiences permits us to talk about the essential, the intrinsic, the basic, the most fundamental religious or transcendent experience as a totally private and personal one which can hardly be shared (except with other "peakers"). As a consequence, all the paraphernalia of organized religions—buildings and specialized personnel, rituals, dogmas, ceremonials, and the like—are to the "peaker" secondary, peripheral, and of doubtful value in relation to the intrinsic and essential religious or transcendent experience. Perhaps they may even be very harmful in various ways. From the point of view of the peak-experiencer, each person has his own private religion, which he

190

develops out of his own private revelations, in which are revealed to him his own private myths and symbols, rituals and ceremonials, which may be of the profoundest meaning to him personally and yet completely idiosyncratic, i.e., of no meaning to anyone else. But to say it even more simply, each peaker discovers, develops, and retains his own religion. . . .

In addition, what seems to be emerging from this new source of data is that this essential core-religious experience may be embedded either in a theistic, supernatural context or in a nontheistic context. This private religious experience is shared by all the great world religions including the atheistic ones like Buddhism, Taoism, Humanism, or Confucianism. As a matter of fact, I can go so far as to say that this intrinsic core-experience is a meeting ground not only, let us say, for Christians and Jews and Mohammedans but also for priests and atheists, for communists and anti-communists, for conservatives and liberals, for artists and scientists, for men and women, and for different constitutional types, that is to say, for athletes and for poets, for thinkers and for doers. I say this because our findings indicate that all or almost all people have or can have peak-experiences. Both men and women have peak-experiences, and all kinds of constitutional types have peak-experiences, but, although the content of the peak-experience is approximately as I have described for all human beings, . . . the situation or the trigger which sets off peak-experience, for instance in males and females, can be quite different. These experiences can come from different sources, but their content may be considered to be very similar. To sum it up, from this point of view, the two religions of mankind tend to be the peakers and the nonpeakers, that is to say, those who have private, personal, transcendent, core-religious experiences easily and often and who accept them and make use of them, and, on the other hand, those who have never had them or who repress or suppress them and who, therefore, cannot make use of them for their personal therapy, personal growth, or personal fulfillment.

APPENDIX E _____

Regarding the gratifying sexual experience, Perls, Hefferline, and Goodman have the following to say in *Gestalt
Therapy: Excitement and Growth in the Human Personality*
(pp. 419-20):

Love aims at proximity, that is, the closest contact possible while
the other persists undestroyed. The contact of love occurs in seeing,
speech, presence, etc. But the archetypal moment of contact is sexual
embracing. Here the actual spatial closeness spectacularly illustrates
the diminution and unconcernfulness of the background because
there isn't room for one: the lively figure looms trying to dispense
with background altogether, and all its parts are exciting. The figure
is not an "object" of the "subject," for the awareness crowds into the
touch. The "distant" senses are made to feel that they are touch
(touching and touched), for a face fills the oval of vision and small
sounds fill the hearing. It is not a moment for abstractions or images

of other times and places; there are no alternatives. The speech is, so to speak, preverbal; what is important in it is the tone and the primitive concreteness of the terms. And the "close" senses, taste, smell, and touch make up much of the figure. Excitement and closeness of contact are felt as one and the same thing; more excitement is simply closer touch. And motion is finally spontaneous.

The vanishing of the body-background is even more remarkable. Toward the climax, the figure is composed of two bodies; the sense of touching and being touched; but these "bodies" are now nothing but a system of contact-situations at the boundary; there ceases to be a sense of physiological organs underlying. Organic pain becomes unaware. Paradoxically, one's own body becomes part of the Thou, and finally the whole figure, as if the boundary were disattached and placed opposite.

This archetypal contact shows also the creativity of the self. At the height of awareness, the experience is novel, unique, and original. But when, at the orgasm, the boundary is "broken" and the self diminishes, one has the sense of a conservative instinctual gratification of one's own familiar body.

APPENDIX F _____

HAZAIAH W. WILLIAMS, ON
"MAN AND NATURE IN AFRICAN CULTURE"

During his visiting professorship, February 25-27, 1970, as
John W. Bailey Lecturer, at American Baptist Seminary of
the West (Berkeley Baptist Divinity School), on "The Black
Church," the Reverend Hazaiah W. Williams, Director of
the Urban-Black Studies Center, Graduate Theological
Union, Berkeley, California, had the following to say about
the synthesis of man and nature in African culture, in which
emotionality is a predominant dimension of experience:

The African emotive experience has to be taken seriously. There
is in the African mind-set an interesting synthesis between man and
nature as over against the western European mind-set that focuses
on rationality. The rational perspective usually deals with life in
terms of utilitarian values. I see a waterfall and think of how much
power I can get out of it: I think of harnessing, using, making do

for me all that God has made . . . using it to my advantage. The black mind-set has as its cultural root another understanding or synthesis of man and nature in which man and nature play together as an expression of the essential unity of God. Therefore, when man in the African culture prepares to communicate, the synthesis is symbolically played out in an animal skin stretched tight across a tree trunk upon which he brings to bear an experience with nature—the rhythmic feelings of the ebb and flow of the ocean, the rhythmic meanings of day and night, the rhythmic sounds of birds calling in the night, the cries of wild animals in the woods, and the rhythmic pumpings of the heart. These rhythms, which are the underpinnings of life as observed by him, he plays out as his means of communication and continues to draw together from the world that God has given to him. In such communication, he probably has a more adequate means of expression than others. We must understand, therefore, that the emotional is as legitimate for authenticating the truth as is the rational.

Such expression occurs in the black church each week. The black church is the only institution that has kept alive the emotive African heritage and celebrated it unashamedly Sunday after Sunday, year after year. And whether one is high Episcopalian or holiness, if he is black he cannot sing a Gregorian chant without a little of the rhythm creeping in.

I recently had a white cat say to me—a doctor of science, on a board on which I serve: "Hazaiah, we'll get along fine in our work together, if you just won't get emotional." I responded: "Emotionality is at least half of my cultural heritage. Therefore, hear me when I get emotional, for emotionality might well be the stream upon which I float my most lucid content." It is the black church alone that has continuously paid tribute to this peculiar, rich cultural heritage of black people. And if you do not believe my thesis is sound, if you are hung up on rationality, try making love rationally. Sex is one arena where emotionality will get it, when rationality will not. The black church must be understood as the institution that not only supported the people in their survival need, but also celebrated openly their cultural heritage. . . . In our so-called high churches, we must be aware that we cannot talk authentically of fulfillment if we persist, in our worship, in cutting the people off from all that is native to them as they try to express the meaning of life. If you would fully understand what I mean, observe—more importantly, participate in–the black church.

APPENDIX G

PERLS, HEFFERLINE, AND GOODMAN,
ON "ROMANTICIZING SEXUALITY"

Regarding the "isolating" or "romanticizing" of sexuality, Perls *et al.*, say the following in *Gestalt Therapy: Excitement and Growth in the Human Personality* (pp. 337-38):

A chief social device for isolating sexuality is, paradoxically, the healthful, sane, scientific attitude of sex education on the part of educators and progressive parents. This attitude sterilizes sexuality and makes official, authoritative, and almost mandatory what by its nature is capricious, non-rational, and psychologically explosive (though organically self-limiting). Sexuality is organically periodical, no doubt, but it is not by prescription that one loves. It was against this isolation that Rank warned when he said that the place to learn the facts of life was in the gutter, where their mystery was respected, and blasphemed—as only true believers blaspheme. It is now taught that sexuality is beautiful and ecstatic and not "dirty"; but of course it is, literally, dirty, *inter urinas et faeces;* and to *teach* that it is ecstatic (rather than to let this be the surprise of an occasion) must,

196

in the vast majority of persons whose aggressions are blocked and who therefore cannot give in themselves nor destroy resistance in others, only cause disappointment and make them ask, "What, is it only this?" It is far better, permitting everything, to say nothing at all. But the so-called wholesome attitude, that turns an act of life into a practice of hygiene, is a means of control and compartmenting.

Of course the pioneer sex educators were revolutionaries; they were bent on undoing the contemporary repression and unmasking the hypocrisy; therefore, they shrewdly seized on all the good and angelic words. But these same words are now a new taboo—"sex is beautiful, keep it clean"—they are a social defense-in-depth. This is why deprivation and the forbidden seem to lead to more intense sexual excitement; it is not that the organism needs these extrinsic aids, but that, in the blocked organism, they prevent compartmenting, they keep open the connections to resentment and rage and the unaware aggression against authority and, at a very deep level, to the desperate risking of the self. For at the moment that one is defying the taboo and running the fatal danger, one is likely to have a flash of spontaneous joy.

BIBLIOGRAPHY _____

Allport, Gordon. *Becoming*. New Haven: Yale University Press, 1955.

——. *The Individual and His Religion*. New York: The Macmillan Co., 1950.

Baldwin, James. "The Uses of the Blues." *Playboy*, January 1964, p. 131.

Barrett, William. *Irrational Man*. New York: Doubleday and Co., Anchor Book, 1958.

Beck, Robert N. "Hall's Genetic Psychology of Religious Conversion." *Pastoral Psychology*, September 1965, pp. 45-51.

Berger, Peter L. *The Precarious Vision*. New York: Doubleday and Co., 1961.

Berne, Eric. *Games People Play*. New York: Grove Press, 1964.

Boisen, Anton. *Exploration of the Inner World*. Chicago: Willett, Clark and Co., 1936.

——. *Out of the Depths*. New York: Harper and Bros., 1960.

Bonhoeffer, Dietrich. *Creation and Fall*. Trans. John C. Fletcher. London: SCM Press; New York: The Macmillan Co., 1959.

Buber, Martin. *Israel and the World.* New York: Schocken Books, 1963.

Bugental, James F. T. *The Search for Authenticity.* New York: Holt, Rinehart and Winston, 1965.

Cabot, Richard C., and Dicks, Russell L. *The Art of Ministering to the Sick.* New York: The Macmillan Co., 1936.

Cohen, Sidney. "The Uncanny Power of the Hallucinogens." *The Drug Takers: A Time-Life Special Report.* New York: Time, Inc., 1965.

Cole, William Graham. *Sex in Christianity and Psychoanalysis.* New York: Oxford University Press, 1955.

Enright, John. "An Introduction to Gestalt Techniques." In Fagan and Shepherd, *Gestalt Therapy Now.*

Fagan, Joen, and Shepherd, Irma, eds. *Gestalt Therapy Now.* Palo Alto, Calif.: Science and Behavior Books, 1970.

Frankl, Viktor E. *Man's Search for Meaning.* New York: Beacon Press, 1963.

Gustaitis, Rasa. *Turning-On Without Drugs.* New York: The Macmillan Co., 1969.

Hall, G. Stanley. *Adolescence: Its Psychology.* New York: D. Appleton and Co., 1904.

Heschel, Abraham J. *Who Is Man?* Stanford, Calif.: Stanford University Press, 1965.

Hesse, Hermann. *Demian.* New York: Harper & Row, 1965.

Hillman, James. *Suicide and the Soul.* New York: Harper & Row, 1964.

Hiltner, Seward. *Sex and the Christian Life.* New York: Association Press, 1957.

Homans, Peter. "Integrating Agency and Communion." Review of *The Duality of Human Existence* by David Bakan. *The Christian Scholar,* Spring 1967, pp. 75-80.

Howes, Elizabeth. "The Contribution of Dr. C. G. Jung to Our Religious Situation and the Contemporary Scene." *Pastoral Psychology,* February 1966, pp. 35-46.

Jackson, Charles. *The Fall of Valor.* New York: Popular Library, 1964.

James, Muriel M. "The Use of Structural Analysis in Pastoral Counseling." *Pastoral Psychology,* October 1968, pp. 8-15.

James, William. *Collected Essays and Reviews.* New York: Longmans, Green and Co., 1920.

———. *Psychology: The Briefer Course.* Edited and with an introduction by Gordon W. Allport. New York: Harper & Row, 1961 (1892).

———. *The Varieties of Religious Experience.* New York: The New American Library, 1958 (1902).

Kepner, Elaine, and Brien, Lois. "Gestalt Therapy: A Behavioristic Phenomenology." In Fagan and Shepherd, *Gestalt Therapy Now.*

Ketcham, Charles B. *The Search for Meaningful Existence.* New York: Weybright and Talley, 1968.

Laing, Ronald D. *The Divided Self.* New York: Pantheon Books, 1970 (1960).

———. *The Politics of Experience.* New York: Ballantine Books, 1967.

Levitsky, Abraham, and Perls, Frederick S. "The Rules and Games of Gestalt Therapy." In Fagan and Shepherd, *Gestalt Therapy Now.*

Louria, Donald B. *The Drug Scene.* New York: McGraw-Hill, 1968.

Lowen, Alexander. *The Betrayal of the Body.* New York: Collier Macmillan, 1969 (1967).

Maslow, Abraham H. *Religions, Values, and Peak-Experiences.* Columbus: Ohio State University Press, 1964.

May, Rollo, *et al. Existence: A New Dimension in Psychiatry and Psychology.* New York: Basic Books, 1958.

May, Rollo. "Religion, Psychotherapy, and the Achievement of Selfhood, I and II." *Pastoral Psychology,* October and November, 1951.

———. "Existentialism, Psychotherapy, and the Problem of Death." In Shinn, *Restless Adventure: Essays on Contemporary Expressions of Existentialism.*

Mitford, Jessica. *The American Way of Death.* New York: Simon & Schuster, 1963.

Muckenhirn, Maryellen, ed. *The Future as the Presence of Shared Hope.* New York: Sheed & Ward, 1968.

Naranjo, Claudio. "I and Thou: Here and Now: Contributions of Gestalt Therapy." Esalen Institute: Paper No. 5, 1967.

———. "Present-Centeredness: Technique, Prescription, and Ideal." In Fagan and Shepherd, *Gestalt Therapy Now.*

Peake, Arthur S., ed. *The People and the Book.* Oxford: Clarendon Press, 1925.

Pedersen, Johannes. *Israel: Its Life and Culture.* 2 vols. London: Oxford University Press, 1926.

Perls, Frederick S. *Ego, Hunger and Aggression.* London: George Allen and Unwin, 1947; Vintage Book; New York: Random House, 1969.

———. "Four Lectures." In Fagan and Shepherd, *Gestalt Therapy Now.*

———. *Gestalt Therapy: Excitement and Growth in the Human Personality.* New York: Julian Press, 1969 (1951).

———. "Gestalt Therapy and Human Potentialities." Reprinted from *Exploration in Human Potentialities,* comp. and ed. Herbert A. Otto. Springfield, Ill.: Charles C. Thomas, 1966. Distributed by Esalen Institute.

———. *Gestalt Therapy Verbatim.* Lafayette, Calif.: The Real People Press, 1969.

———. *In and Out the Garbage Pail.* Lafayette: The Real People Press, 1969.

———. "Morality, Ego-Boundary and Aggression." *Complex,* no. 9 (1955), pp. 42-51.

———. "Theory and Technique of Personality Integration." *American Journal of Psychotherapy,* II (1948), 565-86.

———. "Workshop Vs. Individual Therapy." *Journal of the Long Island Consultation Center,* Fall 1967, pp. 13-17.

Perls, Laura. "Notes on the Psychology of Give and Take." *Complex,* no. 9 (1953), pp. 24-30.

———. "One Gestalt Therapist's Approach." In Fagan and Shepherd, *Gestalt Therapy Now.*

Polster, Erving. "A Contemporary Psychotherapy." *Psychotherapy: Theory, Research and Practice,* February 1966, pp. 1-6.

Pruyser, Paul. *A Dynamic Psychology of Religion*. New York: Harper & Row, 1968.

Robinson, H. Wheeler. "Hebrew Psychology." In Peake, *The People and the Book*.

Salzman, Leon. "Types of Religious Conversion." *Pastoral Psychology*, September 1966, pp. 8-20.

Sartre, Jean-Paul. *Existential Psychoanalysis*. Trans. and with an introduction by Hazel E. Barnes. New York: Philosophical Library, 1953.

Schaldenbrand, Mary. "Time, the Self, and Hope." In Muckenhirn, *The Future as the Presence of Shared Hope*.

Shepherd, Irma. "Limitations and Cautions in Gestalt Therapy." In Fagan and Shepherd, *Gestalt Therapy Now*.

Shinn, Roger, ed. *Restless Adventure*. New York: Charles Scribners' Sons, 1968.

Shostrom, Everett L. *Man, the Manipulator*. Nashville: Abingdon Press, 1967.

Snyder, Ross. *Inscape*. Nashville: Abingdon Press, 1968.

Tiebout, Harry M. "Conversion as a Psychological Phenomenon." *Pastoral Psychology*, April 1951, pp. 28-34.

Van Dusen, Wilson. "Existential Analytic Psychotherapy." *The American Journal of Psychoanalysis*, XX (1960), pp. 35-40.

Winter, Gibson. *Love and Conflict*. New York: Doubleday and Co., 1958.

INDEX

Body AND Soul